Lightning Strikes

Ground crew apply the name 'Lightning Strikes' and its cartoon illustration to the nose of 42-3073, April 1943. (by Steve Ridgway)

FORTUNES OF WAR

Lightning Strikes

THE STORY OF A B-17 BOMBER

ANDY HARTLES

CERBERUS

First published in 2003

PUBLISHED IN THE UNITED KINGDOM BY;
Cerberus Publishing Limited
Penn House
Leigh Woods
Bristol BS8 3PF, United Kingdom
Tel: ++44 117 974 7175
Fax: ++44 117 973 0890
e-mail: cerberusbooks@aol.com

British Library Cataloguing in Publication Data.
A catalogue record for this book is available from the British Library.

ISBN 1 84145 034 0

PRINTED AND BOUND IN GREAT BRITAIN.

'It is like writing history with lightning
– and my only regret is that it is all so terribly true'.

Thomas Woodrow Wilson
28th President of the United States

To all the crews of '073
and to the many thousands like them
this book is respectfully dedicated.

Contents

Acknowledgments		*8*
Sources		*9*
An Echo In Time		*11*
Introduction		*13*

CHAPTER ONE	INSPIRATION	15
CHAPTER TWO	CONCEPTION	20
CHAPTER THREE	ACCOMMODATION	23
CHAPTER FOUR	CONSTRUCTION	28
CHAPTER FIVE	BAPTISM	38
CHAPTER SIX	LOGISTICS	45
CHAPTER SEVEN	SEPTEMBER	57
CHAPTER EIGHT	OCTOBER	64
CHAPTER NINE	NOVEMBER	73
CHAPTER TEN	DECEMBER	94
CHAPTER ELEVEN	JANUARY	106
CHAPTER TWELVE	FEBRUARY	119
CHAPTER THIRTEEN	LAST MISSION	129
CHAPTER FOURTEEN	POSTSCRIPT	139
APPENDIX	THE MISSIONS & CREWS OF 42-3073	146

Illustrations	*between pages 85-94*
Select Bibliography	*174*

Acknowledgments

The author gratefully acknowledges the assistance given by the following persons over the past fifteen years, without whose interest and encouragement this book would not have been conceived:-

401st Bombardment Squadron: Jack Bowen, Paul Chryst, the late Wilfred P Conlon, Hilary 'Bud' Evers, John C Flinn Jr, Roy J Griesbach, James E McCoy, James H McPartlin and John R Paget.

91st Bombardment Group: Don Freer (322 BS), Joe Harlick (324 BS), Whitmal W. Hill (441 SD), Asay B Johnson (324 BS), Philip G Mack (323 BS), Earl G Pate Jr (324 BS) and G William Potter (324BS).

91st Bombardment Group Memorial Association: Gerry Asher, Ray Bowden, Roger Freeman, Lowell Getz, Vince Hemmings, Mrs Joan Kirwan, Phil Starcer and Mrs Bev White.

United States of America: The late Jeff Ethell, Merle Olmsted (357 FG),Mrs Mai Parsons, Lorieta Pierce and the late Mrs Inice Pierce.

United Kingdom: R W Ayres (Air Transport Auxiliary), Basil Frost (Rougham Tower Assn), Cliff Hall (94 BG Assn), Richard Howes, Ray Jude (East Anglian Aviation Society), the late Grahame Mills (ATA), Bernard Morey (BOAC),Ted Nevill, Steve Pena (EAAS), Seimon Pugh-Jones, Steve Ridgway, Peter Roberts (EAAS), Eric Viles (ATA), Ken Wakefield, Dave Walker, Alan Ward (ATA) and Dave Williams.

Sources

In addition to many published works, this book draws heavily on recent research, both original and derived, and on numerous personal accounts, recorded at the time or subsequently by the aircrew involved, some of whom are sadly no longer with us. Much of the factual data used has been found in official records held by the US Air Force Historical Research Agency at Maxwell AFB, Montgomery, Alabama and the US National Archives in Washington DC; in the main these have consisted of field orders, post-mission reports, missing aircrew reports (MACRs), crew loading lists and 401st Squadron war diary entries. The latter especially contain a wealth of detail and paint a vivid picture of the unit's day-to-day activities, particularly in the period prior to the administrative changes of January 1944. Where ranks are given, they are those held at the time of the event described.

In some areas the results of this latest study are at odds with previously published material. The author has done his best to resolve ambiguities or contradictions as they have arisen, and believes this to be the fullest possible record of the life and times of 'Lightning Strikes'. Any errors of interpretation which may remain are entirely his responsibility. The few inconsistencies which have been found are of a minor nature and are a testimony to the diligence of the squadron 'historical officers' – Captain Davison and Lieutenants Nilson and Albidress – and to the recollections of the aircrews, even through the fog of war.

The 401st seems to have been blessed with the services of an unusually high number of chroniclers. Little has been added to their accounts, save to put them into an operational context; for the most part, the facts speak for themselves.

Inevitably after the passage of sixty years, memories are starting to fade and there are already many aspects of this story which, despite careful research, will probably never be known. Of the young aircrew who flew with '*Lightning Strikes*' in 1943-44, those who survived now belong to a band of fine old gentlemen, but time is steadily thinning their ranks. It has been a privilege to hear their stories.

An Echo In Time

It was a clear autumn day in southern England. Without warning, the emergency radio channel crackled into life.

'Aircraft approaching, running low on fuel. Diverting to Whitchurch, for emergency landing.'

Within minutes, crash crews were taking up positions alongside the runway, their eyes scanning the sky to the east for the incoming aircraft.

In the cockpit, three miles from the airfield, the pilot and co-pilot began to run through their landing checks. They were only too well aware of the consequences should their fuel run out before they reached the runway; immediate loss of power and an unstoppable glide to a crunching collision with the ground – if they were lucky. The risk of an explosion from rupturing petrol tanks was high. With one eye on the gauges and one eye on the runway, the pilots counted off the distance as the aircraft sank steadily over the meadows towards the airfield boundary.

Three hundred feet – two hundred – one...

And then the relief as their wheels thumped onto the tarmac and their aircraft settled into its landing run, no longer airborne.

As they rolled to a halt the pilot and co-pilot allowed themselves a moment of reflection before giving their attention to the waiting emergency crews. Their services would not be needed now – this aircraft and its crew had survived to fly again.

But this was no warplane and the skies were peaceful on that autumn afternoon. Whitchurch airfield had been closed for nearly forty years; only its runway still remained, now hemmed in by houses and factories. The date was 1993 and the aeroplane was a Cessna 152, en route to the new Bristol Airport at Lulsgate.

But at least one of the bystanders was aware that this was not the first aircraft to seek refuge on the runway at Whitchurch. In a strange echo of history, events which had happened fifty years before were repeating themselves; and in 1943 the aircraft in trouble had been a bomber – a B-17 called '*Lightning Strikes*'.

Introduction

During the course of her operational career, the Boeing B-17 Flying Fortress carved out a reputation for toughness and reliability that was second to none, and in so doing earned the heartfelt gratitude of thousands of airmen, which endures to this day. If popularity with her crews is a measure of an aircraft's greatness, then the B-17 must rank among the very best. More than any other aeroplane, the B-17 came to symbolise the Allied daylight air offensive in Europe, and pictures of their massed formations drawing vapour trails across the sky are amongst the most enduring images of World War II. Graceful in flight and sturdy in construction, the B-17 was the first of its generation of bombers to enter military service.

Although relatively unsophisticated by the today's standards, the Boeing bomber was in its time among the most advanced warplanes in the world. First flown in 1935, the B-17 was a product of America's defence policy of the 1930's. Originally conceived as a piece of flying artillery to intercept and destroy seaborne aggressors in the oceans surrounding her shores, America's most famous aircraft would eventually achieve fame fighting a very different war in the skies over Europe.

This is the story of one such aeroplane, the hundred or so men who flew in her and the part they played in the world's greatest aerial campaign, told wherever possible in their own words. None of the characters are famous in the wider sense, and almost sixty years have passed since the historic events in which they took part. The aeroplane which would come to be known as *'Lightning Strikes'* started life in California on the West Coast of

America in December 1942, but would soon be ranging the length and breadth of Western Europe.

From start to finish her story lasts little more than a year, but into that brief span is packed enough triumph and tragedy to last a lifetime.

But what was the chain of events which brought '*Lightning Strikes*' and thousands of her kind to England, and who were the men who came with her to fly and fight so far from home?

CHAPTER ONE

INSPIRATION

At the end of World War I, air power was still in its infancy, but certain far-sighted observers had seen enough of its effects on the course of that conflict to realise that a new military weapon had come into existence.

Men such as Lord Trenchard in Britain, General Giulio Douhet in Italy and, most famously, General 'Billy' Mitchell in the USA, all of whom had commanded flying units in World War I, were convinced that air power had the potential to exert a decisive influence on the outcome of future conflicts and were prepared to say so publicly. It was envisaged that strategic air power would allow the waging of a new kind of warfare in which an air force could, in the words of a Royal Air Force memo of 1928, 'pass over the enemy navies and armies, and penetrate the air defences and attack direct the centres of production, transportation and communication from which the enemy war effort is maintained'.

Understandably, such radical ideas did not find favour with the orthodox leaders of the senior services who had not the vision to foresee a time when an air offensive would be as potent as traditional forms of warfare. Their methods, as so often, were more suited to fighting the last war than the next.

Despite having arranged a series of set-piece demonstrations in 1921, in which successively a German U-boat, a destroyer, a cruiser and finally a 27,000 ton battleship were sunk off the Virginia Capes by bombs dropped from primitive Martin MB-2 biplane bombers, in full view of the US Atlantic Fleet and an audience of watching officials, Mitchell was eventually court-martialled in 1925 for his persistently outspoken criticism of the US air administration; he was suspended in rank and pay, and relieved of all duties. The court, it was explained, was 'thus lenient because of the military record of the accused in the World War'.

Not surprisingly, in the following year Mitchell resigned his commission in the US Army Air Corps, as it then still was. In retirement, Mitchell wrote five books and hundreds of articles; taken together they reveal an astonishingly accurate insight into the future of air power. But perhaps his most important legacy was the part he had played in shaping the thinking of other officers who had served with him – men such as Henry 'Hap' Arnold, Ira Eaker and Carl Spaatz – all of whom would one day hold senior command positions in the United States Army Air Force.

Mitchell died in 1936, and thus did not live to see the morning of Sunday December 7th 1941, when in the space of less than two hours, five battleships were sunk and three more damaged by a force of Japanese bombers and torpedo planes, effectively disabling the US Pacific Fleet at a stroke.

In August 1941 Prime Minister Churchill had crossed the Atlantic on the battleship HMS *Prince of Wales*, to Placentia Bay off the coast of Newfoundland, there to meet President Roosevelt for the first time aboard the USS Augusta. This meeting had resulted in the issuing of a joint declaration, called the Atlantic Charter, being 'a common programme of purposes and principles' which would direct the Allies in their fight to re-establish peace in Europe and also, from an American perspective, indicate an agreement by Britain to put an end to the restrictions of colonialism and permit free world trade. Five months later, these undertakings by Britain were further stipulated as conditions of the Lend-Lease Agreement under which America would supply material war aid to her allies on the basis of deferred payment.

Four days after the Japanese attack on Pearl Harbor had triggered America's entry into World War II, Nazi Germany also declared war on the United States; twelve days later Churchill arrived in Washington, accompanied by the British Chiefs of Staff, for the first of a series of conferences which would be held at places as far afield as Casablanca, Quebec, Cairo, Teheran and Yalta, and would serve as a political backdrop to the conduct of the war. Also present at the White House were representatives of the other twenty-four countries now allied against the Nazi Axis. This conference, code-named '*Arcadia*', concluded on 1st January 1942 with the signing in the President's study of a second Joint Declaration binding all of the signatories together in 'the struggle for victory over Hitlerism'.

In December 1940 Roosevelt had urged America to put the weight of her vast industrial might behind war production and to become 'the great arsenal of democracy'. Now on New Years Day 1942 the White House announced the start of the President's 'Victory' war production campaign which called for the manufacture during the coming year of 8 million tons of shipping, 45,000 tanks, 35,000 guns and 50,000 aircraft. Of those 50,000 aircraft, one was destined to be the subject of this story.

There were two other outcomes of the '*Arcadia*' conference which are worthy of note; the first was the establishment of the Combined Chiefs of Staff acting under the joint direction of Roosevelt and Churchill, with overall strategic control of the forces of both nations. In the words of General George C Marshall, the chairman of the US Joint Chiefs of Staff, this was to provide 'the most complete unification of military effort ever achieved by two allied nations'.

The second outcome was the confirmation of a decision which, possibly more than any other, was to determine the course of subsequent military events for the rest of the war and beyond; it can be summarised in the phrase 'Europe first'. Why is a decision as fundamental as this in shaping the Allies' grand strategy so seldom acknowledged? Perhaps the continuing presence of GI soldiers, sailors and airmen in Europe has become so widely accepted and so embedded in the history of the 20th century as to pass without further comment, but it dates from this decision. Without 'Europe first', there might have been no GI brides, no Glenn Miller UK tour, no Omaha Beach and no US air forces in Britain. Viewed in isolation and with the detachment of the past sixty years, it can be difficult to understand why the United States, having been attacked in the Pacific Theatre, should choose to deploy the greater part of its military strength on the Eastern side of the Atlantic.

The arguments for and against such a proposition had first been discussed as far back as February 1941. General Marshall now presented to the conference a memorandum stating that 'Notwithstanding the entry of Japan into the war, our view is that Germany is still the prime enemy and her defeat is the key to victory. Once Germany is defeated, the collapse of Italy and the defeat of Japan must follow'. The reasons for this policy decision were numerous and complex but, contrary to the view of the US Navy Department, undoubtedly sound.

As General Eisenhower, who was then on the staff at the US War Department and later became Supreme Commander of Allied Forces in

Europe (and later still US President) explained in his book 'Crusade in Europe': *'The United States was the only one of the coalition free to choose which of its enemies to attack first. But if we should decide to go full out immediately against Japan, we would leave the Allies divided, with two members risking defeat or, at the best, struggling indecisively against the great European fortress. Meanwhile, America, carrying the war alone to Japan, would always be faced with the necessity, after a Pacific victory, of undertaking the conquest of Hitler's empire with prostrated or badly weakened allies. Further, and vitally important, it was not known at that time how long Russia could hold out against the Wehrmacht.'*

But how was this policy to be implemented? At this stage of the war, the Allies were still in retreat on almost every front; it was clearly going to take many months to train, equip and transport adequate forces before any major seaborne offensives could be mounted. At the *'Arcadia'* conference, it had been generally accepted that it was unlikely that the Allies would be able to carry out a successful invasion of Europe until at least 1943, despite Russian demands to the contrary. In the event, it was not to be possible until a further year beyond that.

In 1938 Henry 'Hap' Arnold, a long-time supporter of Mitchell's views on the future of air power, and now a Major-General, had been appointed chief of the US Army Air Corps. In January 1939 President Roosevelt, alarmed at Germany's expansion into Austria and Czechoslovakia, and foreseeing the possibility of US involvement in Europe, had informed Congress that the United States' existing air forces were 'so utterly inadequate that they must be immediately strengthened'. A budget of 300 million dollars was earmarked, and a target figure of 5,500 aircraft was set for 1941.

In the spring of that year, discussions had taken place in London between American and British representatives as to the form military co-operation might take in the event of future US involvement in the European war. It was decided that American bombers would be based in Britain to act 'in collaboration with the Royal Air Force against German military power at its source'.

The seeds planted by Mitchell in 1921 were about to bear fruit.

In June 1941, following reorganisation, Arnold's post was redesignated as that of overall commander of the newly-established United States Army Air Forces. Now at the *'Arcadia'* conference Arnold recommended the execution of Air War Plans Division-1, a prewar plan which proposed a sustained air offensive against Germany of six months duration by a force of four thousand bombers, aimed at 154 specific industrial and transport targets, thereby destroying Germany's capability to continue the war and creating the conditions for a successful Allied invasion. Furthermore, the planners had recognised that the destruction of the German air force would be an essential part of this process.

In any case, the events at Pearl Harbor had rendered all other American war plans temporarily uncertain; the air plan was approved by the President as a basis for the production of a force of 5,000 heavy bombers plus an equal number in reserve. The die was cast.

CHAPTER TWO

CONCEPTION

On 8th August, 1934, in the light of the worsening international situation, the US Army Air Corps Material Division invited aircraft manufacturers to tender for the production of a new type of multi-engined monoplane bomber capable of carrying a ton of bombs over 2,000 miles at a speed of 220 mph. Although it was intended to defend America against an attacking naval fleet, the supporters of strategic bombing were not slow to realise that such an aircraft would also have great potential for their purpose.

The Boeing Airplane Company had been building aeroplanes at its factory at Seattle in the north-west of the United States since the 1920s. It had traded well with a series of naval fighters and advanced commercial types, but in 1934 business was slow. A vice-president of the company, Clairmont J Egtvedt, had been present at some of the ship-bombing demonstrations of the 1920s and had been deeply impressed by the challenge they posed. Boeing's board of directors now decided to compete for the bomber contract, as did those of the Douglas Aircraft Company and the Glenn L Martin Company. Unlike the other two manufacturers, however, Boeing's design team opted for an innovative four-engine layout in order to achieve the necessary power. The Model 299, as the prototype was called, drew heavily on Boeing's recent design experience, but with a wingspan of 103 ft 9 in, and at nearly 70 ft from nose to tail, it was huge by the standards of that time. The overall layout was clean and easy on the eye with rounded wings and tailplanes, and a fuselage of tapering circular cross-section leading to a tall single tail fin. When raised, the main undercarriage wheels retracted into the two inboard engine nacelles, leaving sufficient tyre exposed to enable a rolling 'wheels up' landing to be made in case of emergency.

The engines fitted at this stage of development each delivered 750 horsepower, and a crew of eight was envisaged, four of whom were intended to operate guns in dorsal, waist and ventral positions. The prototype weighed 21,657-lb empty and 32,432-lb when fully loaded.

As the subject of Boeing's considerable resources, Model 299 was ready to fly in under a year from the commencement of its design. It was rolled out into public view for the first time at Seattle on July 16th 1935, and first flew twelve days later. The 'Seattle Daily Times' published a photograph of the new aircraft under the headline '15-Ton Flying Fortress' and the name stuck.

Boeing were sure that they had produced a winner, but they still had to convince the Army Air Corps. On 20th August, Model 299 departed from Seattle en route for the AAC evaluation centre at Wright Field, Dayton, Ohio, a distance of some 2,100 miles. The journey was made in nine hours at an average speed of 232 mph; the crew were delighted to find that they had arrived two hours earlier than the AAC reception committee had expected them. Equally satisfying, but more significant for the Air Corps, was the fact that the average speed they had achieved was faster than most fighters then in service.

In the Air Corps trial flights that followed, Model 299 easily exceeded all requirements in terms of speed, range, load-carrying and rate of climb, and proved herself superior to the two opposing candidates.

However, this early promise was soon to be severely undermined; on 30th October the Model 299 prototype crashed on take-off at Wright Field, killing both the head of the testing section and Boeing's chief test pilot. It was subsequently found that the tail-surface parking locks had not been released prior to flight. There was no second prototype in existence with which to continue the air trials, and it may have been this together with its relatively high unit cost of more than $200,000 which persuaded the Army Air Corps to award the contract not to the Model 299, but to its rival at the Douglas Aircraft Company. Nevertheless, the AAC were not so blind to the potential excellence of Boeing's design as to prevent them ordering fourteen pre-production models, with the service test designation Y1B-17 and fitted with more powerful 850-hp engines, for further evaluation.

When delivered in 1937, these were put into the hands of the Air Corps' only heavy bomber unit, the 2nd Bombardment Group, who over the following two years proceeded to demonstrate the transcontinental, and even intercontinental, capability of their new equipment with a series of ever more impressive long-distance and high-altitude flights. By early 1939 the Y1B-17, now fitted with supercharged 1,000-hp Wright Cyclone nine-cylinder radial engines, was achieving a top speed of almost 300 mph, a height of 38,000 feet, and a range of 3,000 miles with a normal bomb load of 4,000-lb. These advances, at a time of deteriorating international relations both in Europe and the Far East, did much to prompt a reappraisal of the concept of strategic bombing. In particular, the reality of air-raids on Nanking in China and Guernica in Spain, together with the limiting effect that the apparent superiority of Germany's *Luftwaffe* was having on Anglo-French responses to her ambitions in Europe, were causing the American authorities to look closely for the first time at their own heavy bomber capability, albeit perhaps only as a deterrent.

It was against this background that, in the autumn of 1939, with its trials completed, the B-17B was gladly accepted for regular service with the US Army Air Corps. The first batch consisted of a mere thirty-nine aircraft; by the end of deliveries in 1945, a total of 12,731 would have been constructed, of which the vast majority were to serve in Europe.

CHAPTER THREE

ACCOMMODATION

On 2nd January, 1942, the day after the conclusion of the '*Arcadia*' conference, Major General Arnold issued an order creating the Eighth United States Army Air Force; its headquarters unit was to be activated at the National Guard Armory in Savannah, Georgia within the month under the command of Major General Carl Spaatz. Also in that month it was announced that the new USAAF VIII Bomber Command was to be based in England and commanded by Brigadier-General Ira C Eaker, a former fighter group commander and another of Billy Mitchell's disciples. Arnold had informed the Texan of his selection for the task with the words, 'I want you to put the fighter spirit in our bomber effort'. In due course events would show that bomber crews required just as much aggression and determination to press home attacks in the face of fierce opposition as did fighter pilots, but often without having the ability to take evasive action or to adequately defend themselves. Eaker was detailed to proceed forthwith to England with a small staff, there to establish a headquarters for the coming 'US Army Air Forces in Britain' and to begin the preparation of the necessary airfields and installations.

In fact, a US Army observer group had been active in the UK since May 1941, and Eaker himself had only recently spent a month there studying the methods used by RAF Bomber Command.

Eaker quickly identified six officers of high calibre to accompany him to England; three of them had been civilians until a few weeks earlier, but had been recruited for their organizational abilities. Among these was Capt.

Beirne Lay Jr, a former Air Corps pilot and now a writer, who later became commanding officer of the 487th Bomb Group and, after the war, with an officer of Spaatz's staff, co-author of the novel 'Twelve O'Clock High'. This is generally acknowledged to be the most accurate fictional representation of life with VIII Bomber Command in the winter of 1942. Also in the team was Lt Col Frank A Armstrong Jr who was to lead the 97th Bomb Group on the Eighth Air Force's first heavy bomber mission and on whose later trouble-shooting of the 97th and 306th Bomb Groups, that novel and the subsequent film of the same name would be based. Another re-enlisted civilian was Capt. Fred Castle who would command the 94th Bomb Group at Bury St Edmunds (Rougham) between June 1943 and April 1944, later being posthumously awarded the Congressional Medal of Honor.

Wearing civilian clothes, this group left the USA in early February and, due apparently to a shortage of military transport aeroplanes, took a scheduled Pan-Am Clipper flying-boat to Lisbon, Portugal via a thirteen day stop-over in Bermuda to await good weather. The Dutch airline KLM operated a regular service to Lisbon throughout the war flying Douglas DC-3s from Whitchurch airport near Bristol, the so-called 'gateway for spies'. This was the only wartime airline route between the UK and the European mainland, and as such the *Luftwaffe* were well aware of it. Whether they knew of Eaker's advance party is not clear, but when out over the Bay of Biscay the pilot called Eaker to the cockpit to point out a twin-engined German fighter in the vicinity. The fighter seemed to have problems of its own however; it did not trouble the DC-3 and was last seen heading towards France with a smoking engine.

Eaker's party arrived at Whitchurch on the afternoon of Friday 20th February and transferred to a de Havilland Flamingo for the short flight to Hendon aerodrome in London, where they were met by a deputation from RAF Bomber Command.

Air Marshal Arthur Harris had only recently been appointed Commander-in-Chief of that force, which had, of course, been conducting limited bombing operations into enemy-occupied Europe since September 1939 but which, under his direction, was about to enter a new and more effective phase of its offensive. On the morning of Sunday 22nd February, the day on which Harris officially took up his new post, he and Eaker met informally and immediately began to display the spirit of co-operation between commanders which would characterize the USAAF's time in Britain. They had previously met in Washington while Harris was stationed there in 1940-41 as head of an RAF delegation to identify suitable aeroplanes to purchase from the Americans. His comments made at that time concerning the battle-worthiness of the B-17, as on some other topics, although accurate, were less than complimentary.

Despite their close working relationship, however, the methods employed by the Eighth Air Force were to remain at variance with those of their RAF counterparts. Central to the strategic bombing offensive envisaged by the USAAF was the pinpoint destruction of specific industrial and military targets by formations of self-defending aircraft. These bombers would of necessity fly at altitudes above 20,000 feet (4 miles high) in order to minimize the effects of anti-aircraft fire, utilizing the new top-secret and highly accurate Norden bombsight to achieve the necessary precision. Such aircraft would need to be sufficiently heavily armed to defend themselves against the fighters which would surely be sent to intercept them, since there were no Allied fighters capable of escorting them over the long distances involved. Close formation flying, based on a separation between aircraft of only half-a-wingspan in all directions, would ensure not only the concentration of bomb strikes on the target, but also maximize the effectiveness of their defensive fire. All these factors required that their operations be mounted in daylight.

Having started its offensive in the early months of the war with daylight attacks against particular targets in a very similar manner to that now intended by the USAAF, RAF Bomber Command had found that their percentage loss rate per operation was too high to be sustained. Contrary to Prime Minister Stanley Baldwin's prediction in 1932 that 'the bomber will always get through', a depressingly high proportion had not been coming back. In the face of these prohibitive losses Bomber Command had reluctantly switched to night attacks and had been obliged to accept the reduction in effectiveness which that entailed. Although it had been accepted that the USAAF's plan for Europe would eventually involve the defeat of the *Luftwaffe*, it had not been fully appreciated that at least air superiority, if not outright air supremacy, was a necessary precondition for mounting a sustained daylight air campaign.

Despite earnest advice from the RAF to the contrary, Eaker remained convinced that such an offensive was not only viable but would ultimately be successful, and that any losses sustained in the process would be a price worth paying. Just how high that price could be, was to be discovered in the months that lay ahead. But despite their lack of combat experience, the Americans brought to the campaign their confidence and enthusiasm and an utter determination to prove their case.

Having renewed his acquaintance with Harris, Eaker set about finding a suitable site for his headquarters. RAF Bomber Command's HQ was located in woodland to the north of High Wycombe in Buckinghamshire, and after some initial difficulty Eaker succeeded in persuading the Air Ministry to requisition the stately Wycombe Abbey girls school, some four miles away, for his use. Commencing on 15th April, the building would serve as the headquarters of VIII Bomber Command for the next three years, under the codename of '*Pinetree*', and latterly as HQ of the entire Eighth Air Force – known as '*Widewing*'.

At the same time, Eaker was keen to know what airfield facilities had been allocated for the units of his command to occupy when they arrived in the UK. Harris had already earmarked eight airfields situated to the north of Bedford, recently constructed for the RAF to wartime specifications. These were duly inspected by Eaker and approved, subject to certain improvements. Furthermore he asked for 53 further airfields to be completed by the end of 1942, by which time the USAAF planned to have twenty heavy bomber groups in the UK; but so far none had arrived and the months were passing.

On June 5th, after a dinner with the mayor and council of High Wycombe, Eaker reluctantly agreed to address British service personnel attending a dance in the town. He had few words to say; 'We won't do much talking until we've done more fighting. When we leave, I hope you'll be glad we came'. Eaker was becoming impatient and even Churchill had written to President Roosevelt urging him to ensure that the first American bombers arrived before July.

As America's best heavy bomber, the B-17 was always destined to be the mainstay of VIII Bomber Command. Eaker rightly believed it to be the outstanding aircraft for the job. The B-17's nearest equivalent, the Consolidated Aircraft Corporation's B-24 Liberator, was slightly lighter and faster and hence could carry a heavier bomb-load over a given distance, but was less stable in formation and less resistant to combat damage. Although having flown for the first time only in December 1939, it would eventually equip the Second of VIII Bomber Command's three constituent Air Divisions, with the First and Third using the B-17.

By this time the B-17 had already seen limited operational use in the Pacific theatre (by just 4 bomber groups) and, in even smaller numbers, with RAF Bomber Command in Europe. Its performance in these early operations had been disappointing. In particular, the RAF had reported lateral instability at high altitude, with the aircraft prone to shuddering at the point of bomb release, and insufficient defensive armament.

These shortcomings were rectified in the autumn of 1941 in the B-17E with a major redesign of the rear fuselage to include a new enlarged tail fin/rudder assembly, thus endowing the B-17 with the best-known feature of its profile. Also introduced for the first time in the B-17E were power-operated dorsal (top) and ventral (ball) turrets and a manually operated tail gun position. With the exception of the nose gun, all armament was uprated from 0.3 to 0.5 inch calibre, and the crew increased to ten, of whom six were air gunners. With all these changes the fully loaded weight of the E model was close to 25 tons, but despite this its performance continued to keep pace by means of uprated engines and turbo-superchargers. The aircraft was now a far more stable platform for precision bombing and much better prepared to face its sternest test in what American aircrews, borrowing an idiom from the world of baseball, would refer to as 'the Big League of sky-fighting'.

An initial order had been placed for the production of 512 of this improved model; the total of all previous variants had amounted to only 119 aircraft. Some months earlier, in order to achieve the massive scale of production required to equip the rapidly expanding USAAF, responsibility for the manufacture of B-17s was transferred to an organization known as the BVD committee, after the initials of the three companies involved - Boeing, Vega (a subsidiary of Lockheed) and Douglas.

In addition to its plant at Seattle, Boeing opened a second at Wichita, Kansas; Douglas prepared for production at Long Beach, California, and Vega at Burbank, also in California.

When President Roosevelt had launched his 'Victory' campaign calling for the production of 50,000 aeroplanes a year, Donald Douglas had replied, 'We can do it'. Now was his chance to prove it.

CHAPTER FOUR

CONSTRUCTION

On 1st July, 1942, a B-17E nicknamed *'Jarring Jenny'* landed at Prestwick near Ayr in Scotland having flown over 3,000 miles from Presque Isle, Maine in the USA via the Northern Ferry Route of Goose Bay (Labrador), Greenland and Reykjavik (Iceland). The first of thousands of such bombers to reach the European Theatre of Operations, *'Jarring Jenny'* was also the first of the 97th Bombardment Group, which by the end of the month had thirty six such aircraft stationed at Polebrook and Grafton Underwood in Northamptonshire. These were the only B-17Es to be sent to Britain, however, because on 30th May, the first example of the B-17F model had left the Boeing production line at Seattle, to be followed in early June by the first B-17Fs from the Douglas and Vega factories. It was this type, externally similar to its predecessor, but with a maximum loaded weight of thirty tons and in fact containing over 400 detail changes, which would be the main equipment of VIII Bomber Command for the next eighteen months. Its most obvious improvement over the B-17E was the fitting of the broader-bladed Hamilton Standard propellers in order to deliver the full force of its even more powerful 1,320 horsepower Wright Cyclone engines, each of which had a power output equal to that of twenty family cars. By the end of its production run in September 1943, 3,404 B-17Fs had been manufactured; 2,300 by Boeing, 604 by Douglas and 500 by Vega. These were to be followed by an even greater number, 8679, of the final version, the B-17G. Of these production totals, about 5,000 B-17s were lost during the war, the majority of these in Europe between 1943 and 1945.

The first heavy bomber mission of the Eighth Air Force, an attack on railway yards at Rouen in northern France by twelve B-17s, was flown on 17th August, 1942. Having previously stated, 'I don't want any American mothers to think I'd sent their boys someplace where I'd be afraid to go myself', Eaker flew as an observer in the lead aircraft of the second flight, appropriately named '*Yankee Doodle*'. Although, in a taste of things to come, the formation was intercepted by three German Fw 190 fighters, all returned safe home. By the end of September, five bomber groups had arrived in the UK and were variously stationed at the eight airfields originally offered by Harris. Each group in turn was introduced to flying missions against targets in occupied France when their standards of formation flying, navigation and gunnery were deemed adequate for the harsh European combat conditions.

During September four further bomber groups were declared operational in the USA and cleared to join 1st Bombardment Wing in England. Among these was the 91st Bombardment Group (Heavy) whose thirty-five aircraft began to depart for the UK in September, and were mostly installed at Kimbolton airfield, Huntingdonshire during the first two weeks of October. The group had been formed at McDill Field, near Tampa, Florida on 13th May, under the command of the forthright Colonel Stanley T Wray. In common with other heavy bomb groups, the 91st was composed of four Bombardment Squadrons, in this case the 322nd, 323rd, 324th and 401st. Kimbolton was not to the liking of the 91st Bomb Group however. This isolated airfield was one of the first of seventy-five such bases in the east of England used by the US Army Air Force, having been constructed by British contractors to a standard pattern.

The building of these bases represented a vast engineering project, the largest hitherto undertaken in the UK. Each one occupied about two square miles of levelled countryside and was usually named after the nearest village or railway station; three intersecting concrete runways fifty yards wide, the main one aligned with the prevailing wind being 2,000 yards long and the other two slightly shorter, were all ringed by a fifty-foot wide perimeter taxying track some three miles long. Up to fifty dispersed hardstandings of either a circular or loop design were provided for aircraft parking around the edges of the site; behind one of these was a large bank of earth as a backstop for test-firing aircraft guns. Routine servicing and arming was carried out by the ground crews at these dispersals, with bombers only being taken inside one of the two or three hangars for major repairs. On one side of the airfield, usually close to the flying control tower, would be the technical, administrative and communal buildings. The bomb dump and ammunition stores would be situated on the other side of the airfield, as far away as possible from any buildings, sometimes hidden in an area of woodland and often with a separate access road. Domestic accommodation for the normal station complement of 2-3,000 staff would be spread out in the surrounding area, often at some distance from the airfield itself.

In addition to jeeps and trucks for official, and sometimes unofficial, purposes, bicycles were the essential means of transport for all but the senior ranks, on and off duty, and most bases possessed several hundred, their acquisition and disposal giving rise to a thriving trade. As Sgt James E McCoy of the 401st Squadron later recalled, 'I paid fifteen bucks for one to some guy who'd finished his missions, and I sold it for eight bucks'.

The clearing of a typical airfield site would require the removal of eight miles of hedgerow, 1,500 trees and 400,000 cubic yards of soil. Its construction would involve the laying of 640,000 square yards of concrete, fifty miles of drains and conduit, ten miles of roadway and 4.5 million bricks in 400 buildings. The average cost of one such airfield was then £1 million; the peak of construction was in 1941 when 125 new airfields were completed in the UK, or one airfield every three days.

The impact that the building of these airbases had on the nearby rural communities is hard now to comprehend. In many instances the airfields were sited in isolated parishes as yet without mains electricity where horses were still used to draw the plough. The arrival on their doorstep almost overnight of a virtual town of 3,000 strangers with a fleet of enormous aircraft and vehicles was bound to change the villagers' way of life forever. It was from such quiet places that the airmen would fly out almost daily to take part in world-changing events; it is perhaps this aspect of the European air war which most continues to fascinate succeeding generations in the UK. In general, relations between the locals and their new neighbours were cordial; in some cases lifelong friendships were formed.

At Kimbolton, as at many of the hastily built new airfields, conditions were basic. The accommodation consisted of unheated corrugated iron Nissen huts, there was mud everywhere and the weight of the B-17s was starting to break up the surface of the runways. Even before all his aircraft had arrived, Colonel Wray requested that VIII Bomber Command provide a more suitable base for his group. He was instructed to assess Bassingbourn airfield south west of Cambridge, which had recently been vacated by an RAF operational training unit.

Bassingbourn was a very different proposition from Kimbolton; opened in 1938 it had been built by John Laing and Son Ltd to comfortable pre-war standards as part of the RAF expansion scheme, with centrally heated buildings, permanently constructed of brick and concrete. Like many airfields of its time, it was situated in open farmland with its main entrance alongside a major road, in this case the A14 'Ermine Street' north of Royston. It had four huge hangars arranged in a crescent adjoining the flying area, with tree-lined roadways and permanent accommodation for 3,000 personnel. A rear gate lay at the end of a lane running through North End in the village of Bassingbourn, past the 'Pear Tree' public house.

Colonel Wray visited the airfield on 13th October, and was so impressed by what he saw that he decided to take possession of the base forthwith, without waiting for official clearance. He ordered his squadron commanders to prepare to move immediately and at dawn on the following day, the 91st began to arrive at Bassingbourn. Whether or not VIII Bomber Command approved of this fait accompli is not clear, but the move was confirmed by a written order on 19th October, and 'The Ragged Irregulars' remained in residence there for the rest of the war. Bassingbourn, designated USAAF Station 121, soon became known as 'The country club of the ETO' - few other US bases offered such luxury. Through the work of the 91st's public relations officer Major Carlton Brechler, and also its proximity to London, Bassingbourn was often visited by journalists and war correspondents and hence there is no shortage of literary and photographic records of the 91st's activities. In May 1943, Capt. Bob Morgan's crew of the 324th Squadron became the first in the Eighth Air Force to complete the twenty-fifth and final mission of their tour, an event which was recorded as it happened in William Wyler's famous documentary film *'The Memphis Belle'* resulting in plenty of cinematic coverage for the group. In time, much of Wyler's action footage would be seen again, spliced into a number of post-war feature films, bringing even greater public exposure to aircraft bearing the markings of the 91st. King George VI and Queen Elizabeth, General Eisenhower, Bob Hope and Bing Crosby, Glenn Miller, Jimmy Cagney and Clark Gable were all visitors to Bassingbourn at various times during the war.

Having settled into their new base the 91st embarked on a programme of training in formation flying, air gunnery and navigation as they applied in the adverse weather conditions of the ETO. At this stage orders were received that every effort would be 'directed to obtaining the maximum destruction of the submarine bases in the Bay of Biscay' in order to support the Allies' then most critical campaign in the Battle of the Atlantic, where German submarines were threatening Britain's vital supply routes. These targets were also appropriate to VIII Bomber Command's stage of development since they required only short incursions into enemy airspace, largely within the range of the available escort fighters, British Spitfires and twin-tailed Lockheed P-38 Lightnings.

However, in the months of September and October poor weather prevented VIII Bomber Command's anti-submarine campaign from getting fully into its stride with only seven missions being flown.

Finally, on 7th November, the 91st itself was able to make a start when fourteen B-17s from the 322nd and 324th Squadrons took part in a mission to Brest in western France. This series of missions continued for the rest of the autumn, with the U-boat pens at Saint Nazaire, Lorient and La Pallice all being visited before the end of the year.

By December 1942 the Douglas factory at Long Beach was well into the production of its fifth batch of B-17Fs, having already produced almost 100 such aircraft.

Two thirds of the workers in the plants were women who were often portrayed in wartime newsreels as 'Rosie the Riveter'. Urged on by American flags and patriotic slogans like 'America will win with wings' and 'Avenge December 7', the workforce put in long hours on the production line turning sheets of shiny twenty-four gauge aluminium alloy into bombers. Although many had no previous experience of factory work, it was found that the women could drill and rivet just as well as the men, and in fact their touch was often more suited to the light metals used in aircraft construction. Sometimes they would write their names inside the aeroplanes, or leave messages and even telephone numbers, to be found later by the aircrews. At peak production the three companies involved were together producing 130 Fortresses a week; Boeing's Seattle plant eventually achieved the record output, with sixteen aircraft in a day. Between 1939 and 1945, 325,000 aircraft were built in the United States, more than the outputs of Britain, Germany and Japan combined. Of these, 36,000 were four-engined bombers or transports. America had indeed become the 'great arsenal of democracy' that Roosevelt had intended.

Towards the end of the month, the assembly of Douglas' 110th B-17 airframe was started on their production line under constructor's number 8009, the thirty-fifth and last of block B-17F-20-DL. The official record of this aircraft begins on 14th January, 1943, when she was certified complete and signed over to the US Army Air Forces inventory with the serial number 42-3073.

The serial numbers of US aircraft were composed of two digits denoting the fiscal year in which its production batch had been ordered, followed by a four or five digit sequential number allocated to that particular airframe within that year. Hence 42-3073 was aircraft number 3073 (of all types) ordered in the year 1942, this number remaining with the aircraft for all of its service life. The number appeared in full stencilled on the aircraft's data panel forward and to the left of the cockpit, together with details of the aircraft's model/block number, crew weight and fuel grade. It was also visible painted in large numerals across the tail fin but in abbreviated form, the first digit and the hyphen being omitted, thus appearing as '23073'. For the majority of routine operational purposes this number was again shortened to the 'last three', in this case '073, although for some official squadron records such as crew loading lists the serial number was quoted in full.

In addition, when taken into squadron use each aircraft was allocated a three letter recognition code which was usually painted along the side of the fuselage, the first two letters denoting the squadron, and the third letter being individual to that aircraft within the squadron. Either this code letter following a squadron codeword, or the aircraft's last three prefixed by the word 'Army' would form that aircraft's radio callsign.

Far more important, as far as the air and ground crews were concerned, was the aircraft's name. Almost without exception, US Army Air Force aeroplanes whether bombers, fighters, transports or trainers were given an unofficial nickname by their crews, usually in the form of some sort of eye-catching illustration or title painted on the aircraft's nose; in everyday use on the squadron and amongst the crews, the aircraft would be known by this name rather than by its serial number or code letter.

The names and their accompanying pictures could be amusing or warlike, patriotic, outrageous, or just plain obscure, reflecting some private joke or catchphrase known only to the crew. Sometimes the words or artwork might have more than one meaning to escape official censorship. Some were little more than rough sketches, while others were beautifully painted by artists of real talent, such as Bassingbourn's Corporal Anthony L Starcer. In part, the act of naming was intended to mark out that particular aircraft as being distinct from the rest, with her own individual personality, and in part to create a mascot to bring good luck to the crews like the figurehead on a sailing ship. Whatever the reason, these nose-art pictures acted as morale-boosters and became a familiar sight in the air and on the ground. In many cases aircraft's names were chosen by the ground crews, who spent far more time with the aircraft than the aircrews did and, and looked upon them as their own property to be used by the flyers from time to time on the understanding that they would do their best to take care of them. After all, at the end of a successful tour the aircrew would be going home, while the ground crews and their machines might remain for the duration. In some cases, this tradition extended to giving a replacement aircraft the same name as its missing predecessor but with the addition of a numeral (2nd, 3rd, etc.) or a tag such as '*Chief Sly's Son*' or '*Bomb Boogie's Revenge*'.

In June 1943, the writer John Steinbeck, then working as a war correspondent for the New York Herald Tribune, wrote an article entitled '*A Plane's Name*' concerning the value of nose-art, in this case '*Mary Ruth*', one of the forerunners of '073.

> '*This crew did not name or come over in the Mary Ruth. On the nose of this ship her name is written, and under it 'Memories of Mobile'. But this crew does not know who Mary Ruth was, nor what memories are celebrated. She was named when they got her, and they would not think of changing her name. In some way it would be bad luck.*
>
> *A rumor has swept through the airfields that some powerful group in America has protested about the names of the ships and that an order is about to be issued removing these names and substituting the names of towns and rivers. It is to be hoped that this is not true. Some of the best writing of the war has been on the noses of bombers. The names are highly personal things, and the ships grow to be people. Change the name of Bomb Boogie to St Louis, or Mary Ruth of Mobile Memories to Wichita, or the Volga Virgin to Davenport, and you will have injured the ship. The name must be perfect and must be approved by every member of the crew. The names must not be changed. There is enough dullness in the war as it is*'.

Although outwardly identical in design to thousands of others, every aeroplane seemed to have characteristics of its own. Some were quicker than others, some slower. Some rode the air sweetly and evenly, others needed a firm hand at the controls. Despite the grievous damage she suffered in her career, '073 came to be known as a steady and dependable ship.

After completing her air tests, on 4th February, '073 was delivered to the Cheyenne Modification Centre operated by United Airlines in Wyoming, the first of a number of such Air Force depots throughout the USA, for fitting out with her military equipment up to the current combat standard.

But the most significant piece of equipment which could have been fitted to '073 had already been omitted from her, by design, on the production line. '073 was the last Douglas aircraft produced with the standard fuel capacity of 1,700 US gallons; henceforth, starting with the very next airframe on the production line, all their subsequent B-17s were manufactured with an extra nine rubberized self-sealing fuel cells in each wing, thereby giving an additional capacity of 1,080 US gallons. This engineering change was introduced in response to concerns over the B-17's tactical radius of action and had the effect of almost doubling it to 650 miles, thus causing the extra cells to be nicknamed 'Tokyo' tanks in the belief that they would give the USAAF sufficient range to make attacks on Japan. While this may or may not have been true, it theoretically placed all of Germany within the range of the B-17s in England.

But this improvement brought its own problems; if the B-17 can be said to have had a weakness, it was its susceptibility to fire. When aircraft with the extra tanks went into action in 1943 it was noticed that they were more vulnerable to explosions in the outer wing when residual petrol fumes were ignited by enemy fire, a problem which persisted until an effective venting system was devised. In this respect at least, the early B-17Fs were more robust than their successors.

Nevertheless the absence of these 'Tokyo' tanks placed restrictions on the operational use of '073 and would be a significant factor in her subsequent history.

On the same day that '073 officially joined the USAAF, Roosevelt and Churchill met at Casablanca in Morocco with their respective staffs to review the progress of the war. To reflect the evolving situation in the Mediterranean theatre, General Spaatz was appointed commander of the newly created Allied Air Forces Northwest Africa, and Eaker's promotion to succeed him as commander of the Eighth Air Force in Britain was confirmed. In the absence as yet of any significant results General Arnold learned that Churchill was trying to persuade Eisenhower that the USAAF should abandon the daylight bomber offensive and join the RAF in night operations. Arnold ordered Eaker to travel to Casablanca as quickly as possible, to forestall Churchill by restoring his confidence in the American plan.

Eaker immediately boarded a B-17 and arrived in Casablanca late on 15th January. On the morning of 20th he called on Churchill at his villa and handed him a single page listing all the reasons why he believed daylight bombing should continue. Contained within that memorandum was the now famous sentence, 'If the RAF continues at night, and the Americans by day, we shall bomb them around the clock'. Eaker pressed Churchill further; he wanted support for an intensified daylight bombing campaign against Germany. Struck by his turn of phrase as well as the weight of his argument, Churchill and Roosevelt agreed to extend the time available for Eaker to prove his case for daylight bombing.

The two statesmen also specifically approved the issue on the following day of the much-quoted 'Directive for the Bomber Offensive' in which the combined British and American chiefs of staff outlined for the first time the purposes of the air offensive from the UK; 'Your primary object will be the progressive destruction and dislocation of the German military, industrial and economic system, and the undermining of the morale of the German people to a point where their capacity for armed resistance is fatally weakened', and also for the Eighth Air Force 'to take every opportunity to attack Germany by day, to destroy objectives that are unsuitable for night attack, to sustain continuous pressure on the German day fighter force and to contain German fighter strength away from the Russian and Mediterranean theatres of war'. Interestingly, there seems to have been no expectation that victory in Europe could be achieved through air attacks alone; the intention was to enable the commencement of decisive operations by Allied Forces on the continent.

In a re-statement of the objectives which had been identified some months earlier in a document known as Air War Plans Directive-1942 (AWPD-42), the Casablanca Directive went on to list the priorities of targets to be attacked - submarine yards, aircraft factories, transportation, oil plants and so on.

Since mid-December Eaker had been confident that his force, though still short of aircraft and crews, was now ready to attack targets in Germany itself, but had again been thwarted by poor weather in the target areas. Two of his bomber groups had been abstracted to support the Allied campaign in North Africa and three were still not at full strength; the four complete bomber groups remaining with VIII Bomber Command, had all by now completed at least eight combat missions, and in the case of the 91st considerably more.

On 27th January, 1943, two days after his return from Casablanca, Eaker despatched a force of sixty-four Fortresses and Liberators in the first US raid on Germany. Colonel Frank Armstrong led the mission to Vegesack with the revitalized 306th Bomb Group. Finding the primary target obscured by cloud they bombed the secondary target, the port of Wilhelmshaven. The Americans were intercepted by German fighters on their way home; three of the bombers were shot down.

CHAPTER FIVE

Baptism

During April 1943 a further five bomber groups were declared operational in the USA and cleared to proceed to Britain for service with the Eighth Air Force. Three of these groups, the 94th, 95th and 96th were intended to form the basis of a further bombardment wing of VIII Bomber Command, to be stationed in the counties of Essex and Suffolk.

The final preparation of groups for movement overseas was carried out at staging airfields in the east of the United States; Presque Isle in Maine was the most commonly used, but others existed at Dow Field at Bangor, Maine, and Grenier in New Hampshire. The 94th Bombardment Group had been activated in June 1942, and after the various phases of training, in mid-March 1943 the air echelon of the unit was at Gulfport, Mississippi, preparing to make the flight to Britain. Having so far flown older B-17s intended only for training purposes, the group had now received brand-new combat aircraft for the first time. As was usual at this time, these aircraft had been delivered from the Modification Centres by ferrying crews of Air Transport Command.

During the winter of 1942-43, no aircraft had made the journey to England via the Northern Ferry Route. At the end of March, the 94th were about to make a crossing by the Southern route via Florida and the Azores, but were held up by serious difficulties with many of the engines fitted in their aircraft. These were not in fact Wright-made Cyclones, but engines manufactured under licence by Studebakers. The problems were traced to failure of the piston-rings leading to rapid oil loss; in the climate of the times sabotage was suspected, but not proved. It is more probable that excessive wear had been caused by sand ingested when the aircraft were previously stationed at Salina in Kansas. The disappointed 94th made their way back to the Air Depot at Mobile, Alabama where all of their engines, and in some cases the aircraft, were replaced.

One of the new aircraft delivered for the 94th Bomb Group was '073, and she was officially assigned to the 410th Bomb Squadron at Presque Isle on 13th April. The excitement of the crews at being issued with their warplanes can be imagined; as with other groups, many of the 94th's original complement of B-17s had their nose-art painted on at this stage prior to departing for England. '073 was given the name *'Lightning Strikes'* together with a colourful cartoon-style illustration depicting the figure of Hitler fleeing from a wooden latrine as it is struck by a bolt of lightning. As with many aircraft, we may never know whether the name and picture had any significance beyond its obvious humorous propaganda value; the name may have had its origins in the Florida proverb, 'When lightning strikes there's no time to worry', a sentiment which would apply equally both to '073's crews and their intended targets. Despite its resemblance to some contemporary 91st artworks such as *'Hitler's Gremlin'* (42-3043) and *'Desperate Journey'* (42-3053), it is likely that it was devised by the members of Lt Harold A Johnson's crew to whom '073 was first assigned.

Although it was well-drawn, unusually this nose-art seems to have been applied only to the starboard side of the fuselage; historical photographs show that in most instances nose-art was applied on both sides or, if on one side only, the port side below the pilot's window was the preferred position. The available photographs of '073's nose-art both depict the starboard side, while no decoration is visible on a photograph taken from the port. If it was the artist's intention to paint matching nose-art on the port side of '073, it seems that it was never carried out.

Although she had been allocated to a squadron, and unofficially named, it is not thought that '073 displayed any squadron code letters at this stage. Apart from her nose-art, '073's factory finish of olive drab on the topside and neutral grey underneath was broken only by her tail serial number and blue and white nationality star markings.

Three weeks after their first attempt, the 94th Bomb Group again set out for England, squadron by squadron, this time via the re-opened Northern Ferry Route.

However, facilities were not yet available in the UK to provide theatre training for three new groups simultaneously, so it had been decided that they should be temporarily stationed at other airfields with established groups. '073 departed the USA on 17th April; the first seven of the 94th's thirty four aircraft reached the airfield of the 91st Bomb Group at Bassingbourn on the 18th, with the rest arriving soon afterwards.

But if Lt Johnson's crew thought they were about to take their new warplane into battle, they were to be disappointed; on the 22nd April, soon after arriving at Bassingbourn, '073 was reassigned to the 91st Bomb Group and allocated to the 401st Bombardment Squadron. This move appears to have foreshadowed a policy, which was confirmed in the following two months, whereby any aircraft not fitted with Tokyo tanks were to be concentrated in the groups of the First Bombardment Wing. In due course some thirty such aircraft were transferred from the 94th, 95th and 96th Groups, which received long-range B-17s in exchange; the few remaining replacement aircraft without the extra tanks were also allocated only to the First Wing. These aircraft were restricted to shorter range missions of five or six hours duration, except when temporary bomb-bay tanks were fitted.

The three new groups remained as guests at First Bombardment Wing airfields for the rest of April and into May, and in the majority of cases flew their first few missions whilst under the training of their 'host' group. The 94th Group flew six missions from Bassingbourn, starting on 13th May, but it seems that '073 took no part in any of these. The 94th Bomb Group moved out to their own airfield at Earls Colne, Essex on 23rd May, and later still to Bury St Edmunds (Rougham). Lt Johnson's crew was one of nine from the 94th shot down during their disastrous ninth mission, to Kiel, on 13th June.

There were no survivors.

The past six months had not been kind to the four pioneering groups of the First Bombardment Wing. The campaign against the submarine bases had been inconclusive, largely because the U-boat pens were roofed with twelve feet of concrete which could withstand any bombs then in use. The formations dispatched by VIII Bomber Command over this period had grown in size to an average of 100 or so bombers, but against these the *Luftwaffe* could send some 250 fighters, and this figure was rising. The First Wing had lost a total of 103 bombers in this period, with over 100 others damaged. These losses amounted to two-thirds of the aircraft and crews originally brought to England; on some missions the loss rate had exceeded ten percent, a figure which was regarded as unsustainable. A loss rate of even four percent theoretically gave a crew no chance of completing a tour of twenty five missions (later raised to thirty) and from January onwards the losses began regularly to exceed this figure. In the period up to February 1943, VIII Bomber Command had received only twenty replacement crews, while losses had been three times that. The 401st Squadron alone had lost 115 men, including its commander Major Edward P Meyers, having started its operations in November with only ninety.

On April 17th, VIII Bomber Command made its first attack on the factory of the Focke-Wulf aircraft company at Bremen, manufacturer of their most dangerous adversary, the Fw 190 fighter. The 91st Group was leading the largest formation yet assembled – 115 B-17s. While on their bombing run, the formation was attacked head-on by wave after wave of Fw 190s in what was reported to be the heaviest opposition to date. Sixteen Fortresses were shot down; ten from the low group, who were flying exposed in the so-called 'Purple Heart Corner' at the bottom left of the formation, the favourite target for enemy fighters where losses were usually highest, the other six being the entire low formation of the 91st Group – the whole of the 401st Squadron. Forty-five were seriously damaged.

As yet VIII Bomber Command was still flying largely unescorted by fighters. Republic P-47 Thunderbolts had been introduced at the start of April but would not fly their first bomber escort mission until May and would not have the range to reach Germany until August when the first effective long-range fuel tanks had been developed.

It was in this context that '073 was transferred to the strength of the 401st, but her time for action had not yet come. There now followed five months of inactivity during which '073 stood unused at Bassingbourn. The reasons for this can be deduced from the group's aircraft and crew status returns for the summer of 1943:-

end of:	a/c assigned:	combat crews:	losses in month:
April	42	24	6
May	36	20	9
June	46	18	6
July	40	10	6
August	28	14	18
September	44	18	7

Even allowing for unserviceability and combat damage, it is apparent that during this period the supply of replacement aircraft was more or less keeping pace with the losses sustained, but that for much of that time the number of available aircrews was steadily falling. In an average month there were twice as many B-17s on hand at Bassingbourn as there were crews to fly them. Only towards the end of the summer did the position start to improve. During these months '073 was of course available for training flights or general transport duties, but she is not recorded as having flown any combat missions, and at no time was she shown as being away from her home station. In Washington, General Arnold also was concerned about the slow build-up of VIII Bomber Command and the mounting losses being sustained over Germany.

Rightly or wrongly, at the Casablanca conference it had been tacitly accepted that a cross-Channel invasion of Europe would have to be delayed until 1944. A Combined Bomber Offensive under the terms of the Casablanca Directive, would provide a constructive alternative for the time being whereby the conditions necessary for the defeat of Germany's forces might be brought about. Central to such an offensive would have to be the destruction of the German fighter force, which despite all its losses, had grown by forty-four percent since the United States had entered the war. In particular, the number of fighters available for the defence of Germany was rising sharply, reaching 500 in July, by means both of accelerating production and the withdrawal of fighter units to their homeland.

Knowing Eaker's powers of persuasion, Arnold instructed him to research his proposals for America's part in the Combined Bomber Offensive for presentation to the US Joint Chiefs of Staff in Washington. His paper detailed six target systems selected for attack – four groups of primary targets – submarine yards, the aircraft industry, the ball-bearing industry and oil production, and two groups of secondary targets – the synthetic rubber and military vehicle industries.

In order to achieve significant damage to these six systems, Eaker made it clear that the scale and scope of Eighth Air Force attacks would need to be expanded according to a set timetable; 944 bombers by July 1943 for attacks within the range of escort fighters; 1,192 by October 1943 for targets within 400 miles; 1,746 by January 1944 for missions of up to 500 miles; and 2,702 by April 1944 for any targets within the operational radius. He estimated that if adhered to, this progression would enable the mission of the Casablanca Directive to be accomplished by the spring of 1944.

The Eaker plan was approved by the Chiefs of Staff on 4th May, and at the Allied Combined Chiefs of Staff conference in Washington, codenamed *'Trident'*, it went on to form the basis of the *'Pointblank'* Directive, issued on 10th June. Significantly this directive emphasised that 'the successful prosecution of the air offensive against the principal objectives is dependent upon a prior (or simultaneous) offensive against the German fighter strength' and that 'the reduction of the German fighter force is of primary importance; any delay in its prosecution will make the task progressively more difficult'. With immediate effect the bombers were to concentrate on plants involved in the production of German fighters and their components – including ball-bearings.

Although the Eighth Air Force was not receiving reinforcements at the rate required by Eaker, by July fifteen bomb groups were in service amounting to a strength on paper of 750 bombers. When the effects of battle damage and crew availability were taken into account, however, this translated into an available force on any given day of less than half that figure.

Undeterred, in the months following the issue of the *'Pointblank'* Directive, VIII Bomber Command stepped up its offensive with increasingly frequent missions against the specified objectives, for the first time carrying out simultaneous attacks on several targets. This culminated in the last week of July when, with a period of good weather in prospect, Eaker knew that the time had come to mount the heaviest series of attacks so far on the German war industry. Between 24th and 31st VIII Bomber Command, starting with over 300 bombers, mounted five heavy raids during the course of which sixteen major targets were attacked in what came to be known as *'Blitz Week'*. Despite achieving significant results, the week cost VIII Bomber Command 100 aircraft with ninety crews being lost – the equivalent of ten whole squadrons, or three complete groups. Not surprisingly after the losses of these continuous missions, the strain on the air and ground crews was beginning to show; the Eighth Air Force was stood down for a period of rest and re-equipment.

Operations were not resumed until the middle of August. After several days of cancellation due to bad weather, on 17th, the anniversary of its mission to Rouen, VIII Bomber Command launched 376 B-17s on an ambitious double-strike mission to the ball-bearing factories of

Schweinfurt and the aircraft plants at Regensburg. In the fiercest air battles yet seen, sixty Fortresses were shot down; a further eighty-seven were later scrapped due to combat damage; 550 crewmen were either killed or taken prisoner. Hardest hit were the 91st Bomb Group leading the Schweinfurt-bound force and the 381st flying below them, losing ten and eleven aircraft respectively.

Such was the impact of these losses that VIII Bomber Command was unable to resume operations until 27th August. For the rest of that month and into September, operations were again restricted to short-range missions to northern France, as part of Operation '*Starkey*', a major exercise in the Channel intended to suggest that an invasion was imminent.

With August's losses now made good, on 6th September 338 B-17s were sent on a costly mission to attack aircraft component factories at Stuttgart. Through a combination of bad weather, inexperience and German fighters, few aircraft succeeded in bombing the target and forty-five were lost. Many of the short-range aircraft of the First Bomb Wing, those without Tokyo tanks, ran out of fuel. Eight were obliged to crash-land with twelve more ditching in the Channel, two of them from the 91st; amazingly, from these twelve aircraft, all 118 crewmen who survived were rescued. After this fiasco, VIII Bomber Command turned again to targets in France for the rest of the month.

At this point, the information available to Eaker indicated that the *Luftwaffe* had nearly 800 single-engined fighters stationed in North West Europe plus a smaller number of twin-engined fighters. It was clear that if the daylight bombing of Germany was to be continued, a way would soon have to be found to disable the *Luftwaffe*.

CHAPTER SIX

LOGISTICS

On 13th September, 1943, '073 was absent from Bassingbourn for the first time since her arrival. On that day she had been flown to another airfield some fifteen miles away at Little Staughton in Bedfordshire.

This airfield was the site of the 2nd Strategic Air Depot, the 1st and 3rd being at Honington and Watton respectively. From April 1943 over 4,000 USAAF personnel were stationed there carrying out major repairs and overhaul, mainly of B-17s.

Each depot served the groups stationed in its wing area; in the case of Little Staughton these were the groups of the First Wing. The preparation of aircraft for combat units and theatre modifications were usually carried out at rear echelon Base Air Depots, but during 1942-43 this work was often undertaken by the SADs when it was more convenient to do so than to send the aircraft up the line, particularly where the upgrading of armament was involved. In addition, each combat base had an attached Sub-Depot unit, at Bassingbourn the 441st, who would perform maintenance which could not be done by the squadron ground staff. For day to day repairs, the 401st Squadron occupied the hangar at the southern end of Bassingbourn's row of four.

The scale of the logistical support required to keep the Eighth Air Force supplied and repaired was staggering; all the more so since it was achieved under wartime conditions and starting virtually from scratch.

For example, a deep penetration raid by 500 bombers would consume almost one and a half million gallons of fuel, 1,400 tons of bombs and over four million rounds of ammunition. The original fuel tankage at each airfield was 72,000 gallons, most of which could be used on one mission; second and even third such installations were later added. In the following year Bassingbourn is said to have become the first airfield to receive petrol via a national pipeline system connected to ports as far away as London, Bristol and Liverpool. To put a force of 500 bombers into the air would require a similar number to be held in reserve or under repair, and would utilize 300 tons of maintenance equipment, and spare parts and materials amounting to 7,500 tons. Even so, during 1942-43 the shortage of spare parts was such that it became a common but largely unofficial practice for ground crews to strip useable components from aircraft which had crash-landed, giving rise to the presence of unflyable hulks, or 'Hangar Queens', at most bases.

In order to mount such a mission, the 5,000 aircrew would be supported by an army of 75,000 officers and men in a multitude of supply, maintenance, planning, administrative and specialist roles.

The UK had been enduring wartime shortages for three years; although the British had been unstinting with their material aid, much of what the Eighth Air Force required had to be shipped in from the US. On August 17th, 1942, The Times carried the following article by its aeronautical correspondent, Peter Masefield, which illustrates the American approach to issues of supply:

'Visiting the aerodromes in this country which have been taken over by the United States Army Air Force, as I have been doing during the last few days, one gets the impression of having made an impossibly fast journey to America. At one moment one is driving along a typically English country road, and the next, as if by magic, one is transported...to an aerodrome which is as typically American as Randolph Field, Texas, the equivalent of our Cranwell.

All trace of British occupation has disappeared...The aircraft are American, and so are the petrol trailers, lorries, mobile workshops, bomb trolleys, Jeeps, salvage vehicles, etc...

The Americans are not relying on this country for even the smallest items; they have actually brought with them their own dust-bins – garbage cans they call them'.

As part of the original equipment of the 94th Group and being still in the condition in which she had arrived in the UK, '073 was by now several months behind the times in terms of combat modifications. As the main instrument of the evolving daylight bomber offensive, the B-17 was the subject of more continuous improvement than any other American aircraft. By July 1943 the list of works to be carried out on a production B-17F in order to make it combat-ready contained no less than 101 items. Most of these changes were made in the light of combat experience or to adapt to the extremes of cold and damp in which the B-17 was now being operated. Some of the tasks were minor; the more significant ones dealt with improvements to such items as the ball turret, top turret, radio, oxygen system, electrical generators, hydraulics, bomb release gear and the fitting of armour plate and glass.

The highest priority was given to the modification to be made to the B-17's nose armament. As early as November 1942 the *Luftwaffe* had discovered that much of the firepower of a Fortress formation could be avoided by making their attacks from the front, often spread out in line abreast to divide the defenders' fire, and thereby also increasing the chance of scoring hits on the Fortresses' cockpits, engines and fuel tanks. None of the twenty-seven pieces of armour plating on a Fortress were positioned to give protection from frontal attack. Their pilots and co-pilots were facing straight towards the oncoming fighters at a closing speed of some 500 miles per hour, unable to take evasive action without compromising the integrity of the group formation. Against such attacks the B-17E had only a single hand-aimed machine gun of low calibre which had been replaced by two 'cheek' guns in the B-17F. After experimenting with various single and twin-gun arrangements, VIII Bomber Command settled on a standard modification of an additional belt-fed .50 inch calibre gun mounted centrally in the nose above the bombsight. Despite informing Washington of the urgent need for rectification, it was not until May 1943 that the first B-17F arrived in the UK already fitted with such a gun mount; power-operated forward armament did not become generally available until the B-17G model, with its trademark chin turret, started to reach the Eighth Air Force in September.

With all the facilities available at Little Staughton, the work was completed within two days and by 15th September, '073 had been returned to Bassingbourn and placed in the care of Master Sergeant Bert J Pierce. One of the squadron's original ground crew chiefs, he was a well-known figure, having responsibility for the maintenance of many 401st aircraft during their time at Bassingbourn, and was awarded the Bronze Star for his meritorious service in designing a tool to simplify engine maintenance. At twenty-eight years of age Pierce was older than most of his colleagues and in many ways typical of his kind, the practical men of common sense and initiative who literally kept the wheels of the USAAF turning.

He had graduated from high school in Belfonte, Arkansas but his daughter recalls that he ' *grew up on a farm in Iowa. He was familiar with using and repairing machinery there and when the automobile came into being, he naturally learned about them. The rest of his knowledge was learned at Keesler field in Biloxi, Mississippi where he was sent to Air Mechanics School. After that he was sent to McDill Field in Tampa, Florida for actual training'.*

'Living through the 1920s to 1940s taught my Dad to be inventive, if you don't have what you need to use, make yourself one. It was some sort of a quick release wrench to unscrew the engine bolts. That in turn got the engines off the plane, repaired, and back on the plane faster'.

The ground crews, each of five men, worked outside in all weathers often building themselves small shacks near the dispersals for some protection from the elements.

'Many times he was told to ready a plane for a morning raid. He would be told to give it 'Maximum Effort'. It would sometimes take them all night but the plane was usually ready by the next morning'.

Ground crew chiefs knew their aircraft better than anyone; their duties included taxying aircraft on the ground in the course of maintenance, and they would often accompany the pilot on test flights. *'The ground crews waiting for the planes to come back from a bombing raid was something he remembered well. He said they would count the planes as they flew over the field to land and hope they all made it back'.*

In mid-1943 the writer John Steinbeck visited Bassingbourn for a week and wrote a series of newspaper articles about life on the 401st Squadron.

'Bomber Station in England, July 2 – The ground crew is still working over the Mary Ruth. Master Sergeant Pierce of Oregon is the crew chief. He has been long in the Army, and he knows his engines. They say of him that he owns the Mary Ruth, but he lends her to the skipper occasionally. If he says a flight is off, it is off. He has been checking the engines a good part of the night.

Corporal Harold is there, too. He has been loading bombs and seeing that the armament of the ship is in condition. The ground crew scurries about like rabbits.

Their time is getting short. They have the obscure job, the job without glory and without publicity, and the ships could not fly without them. They are dressed in coveralls and baseball caps.

The gunners have mounted their guns by now and are testing the slides. A ground man is polishing the newly mended nose, rubbing every bit of dirt from it so that the bombardier may have a good sight of his target.

A jeep drives up, carrying the officers – Brown, Quenin, Bliley and Feerick. They spill a number of little square packets on the ground, one for each man. Captain Brown distributes them. They contain money of the countries near the target, concentrated food and maps. Brown says: 'Now, if we should get into any trouble, don't go in the direction of... because the people haven't been very friendly there. Go toward... you'll find plenty of help there'. The men take the packets and slip them in pockets below the knees in their coveralls,.

The sun is just below the horizon now and there are fine pink puff clouds all over the sky. The Captain looks at his watch, 'I guess we better get going', he says. The other Brown, the tail gunner, runs over. He hands over two rings, a cameo and another. 'I forgot to leave these', he says. 'Will you put them under my pillow?' The crew scramble to their places and the door is slammed and locked. The waist doors are open, of course, with the guns peering out of them, lashed down now, but immediately available. The long scallop of the cartridge belts drapes into each one.

The Captain waves from his high perch. His window sits right over the ship's name – Mary Ruth, Memories of Mobile. The engines turn over and catch one at a time and roar as they warm up. And now, from all over the field, come the bursting roars of starting engines. From all over the field the great ships come rumbling from their dispersal points into the main runways. They make a line like giant bugs, a parade of them, moving down to the take-off stretch.

The Captain signals and two ground crew men dart in and pull out the chocks from in front of the wheels and dart out again.

The Mary Ruth guns her motors and then slowly crawls out along her entrance and joins the parade.

Along the runway the first ship whips out and gathers speed and takes the air, and behind her comes another and behind another and behind another, until the flying line of ships stretches away to the north.

For a little while the squadron has disappeared, but in a few minutes back they come over the field, but this time they are not in a line. They have gained altitude and are flying in a tight formation. They go roaring over the field, and they have hardly passed when another squadron from another field comes over, and then another and another. They will rendezvous at a given point, the squadrons from many fields, and when the whole force has gathered there will be perhaps a hundred of the great ships flying in Vs and in Vs of Vs, each protecting itself and the others by its position. And this great flight is going south like geese in the fall.

There is incredible detail to get these missions off. Staff detail of supply and intelligence detail, deciding and briefing the targets, and personnel detail of assigning the crews, and mechanical detail of keeping the engines going. Bomb Boogie went out with the others, but in a little while she flutters back with a dead motor. She has conked out again. No one can know why. She sinks dispiritedly to the ground.

When the mission has gone the ground crews stand about looking lonesome. They have watched every bit of the take-off and now they are left to sweat out the day until the ships come home.

It is hard to set down the relation of the ground crew, but there is something very close between them. This ground crew will be nervous and anxious until the ships come home. And if the Mary Ruth should fail to return they will go into a kind of sullen wordless mourning.

The crews have been working all night. Now they pile on a tractor to ride back to the hangar to get a cup of coffee in the mess hall. Master Sergeant Pierce says:

'That's a good ship. Never did have any trouble with her. She'll come back, unless she's shot to pieces'.

In the barracks it is very quiet; the beds are unmade, their blankets hanging over the sides of the iron bunks. The pin-up girls look a little haggard in their sequin gowns. The family pictures are on the tops of the steel lockers. A clock ticking sounds strident. The rings go under Brown's pillow'.

It was at about this time that '073 received a visit from the painters of the 441st Sub-Depot. Starting in July, all the aircraft of the 91st in turn had received group markings in the form of a large black 'A' in a white triangle high up on their tail fins. Now, working in the open air, they marked up both sides of '073's fuselage with a ruler and chalk and painted four-foot high squadron code letters – 'LL' for the 401st and her individual callsign letter 'A' – in matt yellow over her olive drab camouflage, astern of the red-edged star-and-bar insignias, with the 'A' repeated on either side of the tail fin below her serial number. After a number of changes, by early 1944, 'LL-A's radio callsign became standardized as 'Mutter A-Apple'.

Four previous B-17s of the 401st had carried the individual aircraft letter

'A'. '*Mary Ruth - Memories of Mobile*' was the third of these; she was shot down by German fighters near Huls on 22nd June, along with four other aircraft from the 91st. Eight of her crew survived. The fourth and most recent, 42-3162, named '*Bucccaneer*', also previously with the 94th Group, had been ditched in the North Sea on 12th August, on the way back from Gelsenkirchen, with the crew becoming prisoners of war.

'073 was allocated to the position recently vacated by her predecessor on a loop hardstanding in the 401st Squadron's dispersal area on the western side of the airfield. Except for time in the air or away for major repairs, this was where she would spend the rest of her days.

Soon it would be her turn to go to war. Over the next five months she would be flown on a total of twenty-seven missions by no less than fourteen different crews. Contrary to popular belief, most crews would fly several different aircraft during the course of their tour of duty, depending on which aircraft were serviceable and which was allocated to them.

Lt Wilfred P Conlon flew fifteen missions as a bombardier in the 401st Squadron, two of them on '073:

> '*When bomber crews were trained in the United States, they were trained with the hope that they would stay together as a crew throughout the war. There was also hope that we would fly in B-17s as a cohesive crew. That is what the intention was. However, the reality was that when we got to England, because of the high mortality rate of both planes and men, crews were utilized and mixed up wherever they were needed. That meant that we would seldom fly in a previously assigned aircraft. I probably flew on ten or twelve different aircrafts out of Bassingbourn during my time there.*
>
> *I arrived at Bassingbourn assigned to the 401st Bomb Squadron of the 91st Bomb Group on September 11, 1943. Between September 23, 1943 and February 5, 1944, I flew ten missions with mixed crews. I was fortunate in flying those missions to have as a pilot my original crew pilot named Hilary Evers. I then flew five more missions until being shot down; as we progressed into those ten missions, the crew integrity idea began to disintegrate*'.

In common with the aircrews of the other air forces of World War II, those of the US Army Air Forces were all volunteers, eager to fly. They came in their hundreds of thousands from all parts of the United States, from all kinds of social backgrounds and from all walks of life. Although representing a broad cross-section of American society, they were collectively above average in terms of physical condition, intelligence and motivation. The demands of going to war in the most high performance aircraft of the day required no less; the flying of continuous missions of several hours duration at high altitude in freezing temperatures and in unpressurized aircraft, assailed by enemy fighters and anti-aircraft fire, imposed enormous strains on the human mind and body. For this reason only candidates between the ages of eighteen and twenty-seven were considered for aircrew training. It was not unusual for all the members of a bomber crew to be aged twenty-one or under. Having been rigorously selected for their physical and psychological aptitude, they underwent a thorough training programme at a cost of $100,000 per crew, at a time when a factory worker earned forty dollars a week and a 2nd Lieutenant aeroplane commander received $270 a month including flying pay and overseas allowance. Thereafter, they would embark upon a tour of duty and would continue, often in fear, until either they were shot down or had completed enough combat missions to go home. None knew whether they would be fortunate enough to do so; the random nature of air combat, adverse weather, inexperience, flying accidents and just plain bad luck accounted for many.

In general, the overall picture of VIII Bomber Command's air campaign meant little to these crews; as with all fighting men, their war was fought in terms of their own survival and that of those around them, of missions successfully completed or aborted, of targets destroyed or to be revisited. The vast majority endured this regime through to whatever end awaited them, and in between managed to find some enjoyment during their free time at a combat base. They were different from their Army or Navy colleagues in that they could at least return each night to the comforts of a real bed and a hot meal, and perhaps the pleasures of English country life or a period of leave in London or Cambridge.

Jack Bowen from Carthage, Texas enlisted in the US Army Air Corps in 1941. Although initially trained as an armourer, Jack was instead assigned to a supply group which, after a perilous sea-crossing, disembarked at Southampton in May 1942 as part of the first American contingent to reach the UK. The unit was initially posted to RAF Molesworth in Huntingdonshire, one of the original eight airfields allocated to VIII Bomber Command, and later to Poynton near Manchester, as an advance party to establish Supply Depots for the bomber groups which were soon to follow.

'When I wasn't flying I loved to get on a bicycle and ride through the countryside. I fell in love with the UK. While I was there, it was sort of like home to me. Of all the places I was ever stationed while in the military, the UK was the best.

One day my friend and I went riding late in the day and came upon a pub, I don't remember the name, it was dusk so we decided to stop for a mild and bitter. Much to our surprise the pub had a room adjoining it, where they were dancing and having a party. The man behind the bar told us we should go to the party, which we did. Much to our surprise, as we walked in everyone stood and gave us a rousing reception. It was, to me, a bit embarrassing as I was young and I hadn't done a lot, but we graciously acknowledged their greeting. Then a young lass stood up and sang, 'I'm a Yankee Doodle Dandy'. Man, did I feel good, I felt as though I was six feet tall! Needless to say we drank too many pints before the evening was over. But a wonderful time was had by all'.

Eventually Jack succeeded in obtaining a transfer to the gunnery school at Bassingbourn, in order to return to his proper trade. Not surprisingly he found the course relatively easy and passed with flying colours.

'I was assigned to the 401st Bombardment Squadron, 91st bomb Group and at first flew either ball turret or waist, whichever they needed as I had no crew at this time. While stationed there and flying missions, we would take bicycle rides through the countryside which was and still is lovely. We often caught the bus to Cambridge. One incident occurred while a friend and I went there once. We had drunk a few pints and decided we would rent a canoe (punt). This was our first mistake as neither of us had ever paddled a canoe. The second mistake was when we placed it in the river and started paddling. We were paddling by the campus at Cambridge university and I don't have to tell you what transpired next, yes we flipped over and with our uniform and heavy GI shoes it was hard to swim but we finally made it to shore. Needless to say I have never been in another canoe. I was invited into many homes while there. I had meals with them (wouldn't eat much as I knew everything was rationed). I was treated with the utmost respect and courtesy and tried to repay it in like manner'.

These were high-spirited healthy young men doing their best under great pressure, and if there were occasional excesses, they were surely justified.

'My experiences in England will be remembered by me the rest of my life. I was only eighteen when I arrived and was shot down when I was twenty. People of

England took us into their homes and hearts and I will always be grateful. Those were some of the happiest and, yes, some of the saddest days. I know the people thought we were a little brash and loud but we were really boys trying to become men, and I know that they knew this and we were a little frightened'.

Heavy bomber pilots were required to bear a particularly heavy burden. In addition to needing the strength and skill to operate a large and complex warplane, and often powerless in the face of fighters or flak, the pilot was responsible for the lives of nine other men, and as such was always the aeroplane's commander, regardless of the rank of his passengers, with his co-pilot as his second-in-command. In the case of the lead aircraft in a formation, a pilot of the rank of Captain or Major might well have a Colonel or even General travelling with him as the group, wing or mission commander.

Due partly to the layout of the aeroplane, the pilot and co-pilot also had significantly less chance than other crew members of escaping from a stricken B-17 in a hurry, as did ball turret gunners. It was likely, however, that at some point the survival of the crew would depend on each and every member in turn performing his allotted tasks efficiently. In the course of training and in the heat of combat, the four officers and six enlisted men of a bomber crew would become welded together as an interdependent team, highly protective of one another and often uneasy about flying with relative strangers.

In early 1944, the Army Air Force conducted a study to find out why it was that, despite the appalling casualties, their aircrewmen remained so committed to combat flying. The answer lay in their satisfaction at having worked hard to attain aircrew status, confidence in their training and ability, an absolute conviction as to the importance of their service to their country and, most importantly, an intense comradeship with their crewmates. They cared deeply about each other and whatever they endured, they did so for each other; it would have been unthinkable to let their colleagues down. This team spirit generated enormously high motivation and morale; even today whenever aircrew veterans look back across a lifetime and speak of the young men with whom they served in their formative years, it is evident that they still have the highest regard for their former comrades and a strong sense of pride in what they achieved together.

It is usual nowadays to refer to aircrews as being members of a given Bomb Group at a particular base; although proud of their group, the crews' first loyalty beyond each other was to their squadron, for it was to the squadron that they were posted and it was with others of their squadron that they lived, flew and fought.

'We spent most of our time with our squadron, but you might have a drink with some other guys in the Officers' club; you wouldn't necessarily know which unit they were from'. Lt Don Freer, pilot 322nd Squadron.

The ground crews on whom their lives depended were included within the aircrews' circle of teamwork, and that loyalty was duly reciprocated. Although they were distinct from the aviators, their dedication was recognized and there was great comradeship between the two. During their time with the squadron, the ground crews would see many aircrews come and go, and were always saddened by their loss. In some units it was customary to allow the ground personnel to go along on just one combat mission if they wished, usually after some instruction in air gunnery. Bomber crewmen also felt immense gratitude to the fighter pilots who escorted them. In their turn, the 'Little Friends' admired the courage of the bombers; they understood that their very different roles had a common purpose, that of placing bombs on the target.

In 1943, each bomber group of four squadrons had a theoretical strength of thirty-six crews, although this was often reduced by losses. On any given mission, one of the four squadrons would be stood down, in rotation; of the other three squadrons, one or two crews from each might be on leave or under training. Initially, the intention was for three squadrons each to provide six aircraft for the mission, flying in two flights of three, the group formation thus consisting of eighteen aircraft. This was not always possible and a good deal of borrowing of aircraft and crews occurred in order to make up a usable formation. Later in 1943, when their numbers started to rise substantially, most groups had sufficient aircraft to be able to put up a twenty-one aircraft formation or to make up extra 'composite groups' in partnership with another unit, or even to put up double formations of their own.

Also on September 13th, in order to increase their operational efficiency, the heavy bomber wings of VIII Bomber Command underwent an administrative reorganization into three Air Bombardment Divisions each composed of three Combat Bombardment Wings, with two or three Bomb Groups apiece. The former First Bombardment Wing thus became the First Air Division, with its headquarters at Brampton Grange near Huntingdon, and consisting of the 1st, 40th and 41st Combat Bombardment Wings. The 91st Bomb Group became part of the 1st Combat Wing together with the 381st Bomb Group from Ridgewell and the 351st based at Polebrook, later replaced by the 398th at Nuthampstead. The Third Air Division was composed of bomb groups wholly equipped with the long-range B-17s, and the four B-24 groups made up the smaller Second Air Division which continued to operate separately from the other two.

Each Eighth Air Force bombing mission originated with the nomination of a target selected from the list of strategic objectives, at a daily meeting at VIII Bomber Command headquarters at High Wycombe, based on a report of the predicted weather conditions for the next twenty-four hour period. Once identified, details of the target and the overall mission plan would be transmitted by teleprinter to the three Air Division headquarters where the specific operational details of the mission would be worked out and transmitted onwards to the Combat Wings, and thence to the individual Bomb Groups, in the form of a field order. Every facet of the mission would be covered in the order – targets and diversions, fuel and bombloads, formations and assembly points, routes and timings, altitudes, callsigns, radio channels and fighter support – to ensure that the multitude of components came together at exactly the right time and place for a successful mission. All this was preceded by a telephoned 'alert' to enable the groups to place their crews on standby for the following day.

CHAPTER SEVEN

SEPTEMBER

On the evening of 14th September, for the seventh time that month, the lists of crews for the following day's mission were pinned up on the notice-boards in the barrack block hallways. Four of these previous missions had been cancelled due to poor weather, causing the usual sense of anticlimax amongst the crews – but this one would not be. This time the alert list showed an aircraft number not seen before – 42-3073 – and alongside it were the names of 2nd Lieutenant Robert A Pitts and his crew. It was to be the first mission of the 91st following the failure of Stuttgart – yet another short-range mission to France, in this case a second attack in a month on the *Luftwaffe* aircraft repair depot at Romilly-sur-Seine south-east of Paris, by eighty seven bombers of the 1st Air Division.

Lieutenant Pitts had joined the 401st Squadron during the summer, in the rank of Flight Officer, the nearest the USAAF came to using non-commissioned pilots. On previous missions his crew had flown an aircraft called '*Ramblin' Wreck*' but she had recently spent a week under maintenance at Little Staughton and on this day they were instead taking '*Lightning Strikes*' on her first venture into enemy airspace. It was usual for newly-issued aircraft to be allocated to the more experienced crews; novice crews were obliged to cut their teeth on more battle-worn machines.

The 401st had not yet recovered from its heavy losses during the preceding months, and was able to supply only two of the nineteen aircraft despatched by the 91st Bomb Group. At about halfway through their tour the Pitts crew were by now very familiar with the rituals of breakfast and briefing, before collecting protective clothing and guns, and travelling in trucks out to the aircraft at their dispersals, which preceded this and every mission. Once there, the cycle of checking equipment, of starting and running up engines, of taxying out and taking off in succession, and the laborious process of climbing to height and forming up by flights, squadrons, groups and wings followed the well rehearsed routine. This being an afternoon mission, however, the crews were spared the hardship of being roused from their beds in the small hours to carry out their mission preparations in the pre-dawn darkness. The other aircraft, named '*The Shamrock Special*', was flown by Capt. Harry Lay, one of the senior pilots of the 401st, who would soon become the first pilot in the 91st to complete an extended tour of thirty missions but who was sadly killed after returning for a second tour of duty, on fighters.

The aircraft of the 91st were each loaded with thirty-eight 100-lb incendiary bombs. Others in the First Air Division carried general-purpose high explosive bombs; the range of the mission was sufficiently short that some also carried two 1,000-lb bombs in external wing racks fitted between the fuselage and the inboard engine nacelles. The Second and Third Air Divisions were also in action attacking other targets in Occupied France. The bombers were well escorted by the five available Thunderbolt fighter groups, including the 355th from Bassingbourn's satellite airfield at Steeple Morden, who had made their operational debut on the previous day. Although a small number of enemy fighters were seen, none attacked the 91st Bomb Group.

After encountering some light and inaccurate anti-aircraft fire the First Division passed over its target at 6.48pm Double British Summer Time and released nearly 268 tons of bombs from 23,000 feet. If part of the objective had been to resume operations as painlessly as possible, then it was achieved; all the aircraft of the First Air Division returned home, although seven were damaged and three crewmen wounded. The strike photographs, however, showed that the 91st's bombs had fallen short of the target. Despite the disappointing results, '073 had safely completed her first mission.

The 91st were in action again next day, but '073 was not required to fly again until a week later, on 23rd September. In the interim, four missions had been scheduled and then scrubbed due to poor weather.

This was a significant date in the history of VIII Bomber Command; for the first time two entirely separate heavy bomber missions were mounted in the same day – one in the morning and one in the afternoon/ evening. Early in the day, while most of VIII Bomber Command were assigned to attacks on *Luftwaffe* airfields at various places in Occupied France, half of the First Division, drawn from the groups of the 1st and 40th Combat Wings, were briefed to attack the port of Nantes in western France with the intention of destroying a U-boat supply ship in the harbour. The 91st, led by Major Weitzenfeld with the 324th Squadron, provided twenty-one aircraft of the 117 in this formation. This time the 401st despatched four aircraft, one of which was '073 again flown by Lt. Pitts, but with five new crew members, the others being *'The Shamrock Special'* flown by Captain Lay, *'Ramblin' Wreck'* and *'Sheila B Cummin'*. Flying alongside '073, in *'Ramblin' Wreck'* was a new crew on their first mission, led by 2nd Lt Hilary 'Bud' Evers from South Carolina. Like many airmen, the top turret gunner of that crew, Sergeant John Capron, kept a log of his missions in a combat diary:

> *'After five starts we finally made our first one today. We went to Nantes, France. We were flying in the low group in the diamond position, or 'Tail End Charlie'.*
>
> *Our primary target was one ship in the harbor. The ETA at the target was 0815 and at exactly this time, 'bombs away'. Just a few moments before this, five Fw 190's queued up on our tail. I fired a short burst at the first one as he pealed (sic) off and then was hit in the left arm from a fighter making a head on attack. Don't remember the other four.*
>
> *There wasn't too much flack but it was very accurate. We had trouble with our bomb release and so dropped ours on the secondary target, an airfield.*
>
> *Enemy Aircraft – two probable.*
>
> *Bomb Load – 12/500-lbs.*
>
> *Time – 7 hrs. 35 min.'*

Whereas 'Purple Heart Corner' was the lowest part of the group, on the left of the low squadron, 'Tail End Charlie' was the name generally given to the highest position, on the opposite side of the formation, usually occupied by a novice crew, in the rearmost element of the high squadron. In early 1943 a report by the First Bombardment Wing's Tactical Advisory Board had described the leader of the second element of the high squadron as 'the most difficult position to fly in the formation'.

Lt Bert Stiles, who flew thirty-five missions as a co-pilot in the 401st Squadron, described the reality of formation flying in his classic book '*Serenade to the Big Bird*' which was published after his death on a second tour, flying a P-51 Mustang over Hannover in November 1944:

> '*The strange thing is, from any distance, a formation is always static, and always beautiful. You don't hear the pilots screaming at the co-pilots and the element leaders bitching at the squadron leaders.*
>
> '*Get us out of here', somebody will call up the lead ship. 'We're in prop wash'.*
> '*Can you cut it down a little?'*
> '*Can you pick it up a little? We're stalling out back here.'*
> *Bitch, bitch, bitch.*
>
> *The Group leaders plead with the Wing leaders, and the Wing leaders weave in and out to stay in Division Formation, and the whole 8th Air Force gets there some way.*
>
> *A ground-gripper would never notice a low squadron over-running a lead squadron, or see the high squadron leader chop his throttles and almost pile his wingmen into his trailing edges.*
>
> *From the ground, or to a passenger in the air, it just looks deadly and simple and easy.*
>
> *And actually it is deadly if it's flown tight, and the bomb pattern is compact, and it is simple and easy if you stay on the ball and fly. You can stay in some positions with two throttles, setting the inboard engines at a constant RPM, and moving the outboards a quarter of an inch at a time. You can fly back on the tail end of an 18-ship formation and spend the whole day sliding up on your element leader, punching rudders to keep from over-running him, and pouring it on to catch up again.*
>
> *A formation depends on its leaders. Good squadron leaders and good element leaders make formation-flying easy. Bad ones make it hell.'*

In fact, the weather in the target area was so heavy that the formation became scattered and only forty-six out of the 117 B-17s managed to bomb effectively. Those that did had dropped down below the cloud to 16,000 feet from where they bombed visually, releasing 134 tons of 500-lb bombs with the good results. The port was damaged, with hits being reported on the supply ship itself. Anti-aircraft fire was described as moderate but accurate. Thunderbolts provided the escort as about fifty German fighters made fierce attacks on the bombers. Forty-one aircraft from this formation were damaged, including fourteen from the 91st, but none were destroyed. Thirteen crewmen were killed and eleven injured. In the 401st, in addition to Sgt Capron, Sgt Robert Youker in Captain Lay's crew sustained a flak wound in the shoulder.

Unfortunately, Lt Pitts' crew was one of those which flew over the target area at the briefed height of 21,000 feet, above the cloud layer, and failed to sight the objective. At some point thereafter, due to a combination of the weather conditions and enemy fighter attacks, '073 and another B-17 became separated from the main formation. Shot up and finding themselves alone and without protection Lt Pitts in '073 and 2nd Lt Charles Pinning of the 322nd Squadron in 42-29711 'Chief Sly III' took the only sensible course of action. Unsure of their position, they turned north towards England, knowing that they would eventually cross its coastline. Portland Bill stands on the coast some 240 miles more or less due north of Nantes; after a further sixty miles over the rolling countryside of Dorset and Somerset they came to Whitchurch airfield on the outskirts of Bristol. By this time the two B-17s had flown at least 700 miles since take-off and had been in the air for over six hours. These were of course non-Tokyo tank aircraft and, according to eye-witnesses, were leaking fuel as a result of battle damage. With little fuel remaining there was now an urgent need to find a landing-place, and on sighting Whitchurch the pilots had no hesitation in preparing to land. Lt Pitts took '073 in first, closely followed by 'Chief Sly III'. In addition to being a working civil airport used by KLM and BOAC, Whitchurch also housed No. 2 Ferry Pool of the Air Transport Auxiliary. The sight of the two bombers landing in such a hurry caused quite a stir among the ground and flight personnel. A number of them turned out to watch as '073 and '711 taxied onto the grass beside the runway and parked up. Soon the bombers were surrounded by a crowd of inquisitive onlookers; a camera was brought out and photographs were taken.

ATA First Officer Alan L Ward was one such bystander and in 1996 he recognised himself in the foreground of a photograph taken on that day as 'a hook-nosed gent wearing specs, fifty-four years younger'.

One of the staff of the BOAC's Engineering Department, Bernard Morey later recalled:

> *'From time to time the odd American bomber dropped into Whitchurch returning from an aborted mission due to low cloud over the target and shortage of fuel. On this occasion, two B-17s dropped in at the same time. They had bullet*

holes in the wings and a full bomb load intact. The one and only main runway was 3,000 feet long and 150 feet wide.

Judging by the amount of smoke coming off the tyres it was obvious to the onlookers that something was definitely amiss. After they had come to rest we all trooped down to the aircraft to have a shufty and lo and behold they were fully loaded with bombs. All the racks were fully loaded and I was not at all surprised that the tyres were a little more than warm.

The crews didn't appear to be at all concerned about the babies they had on board, but one thing was certain, they could not take off again with that load aboard. The wings were punctured with bullet holes which probably explained the loss of fuel but there were no casualties.

In a very short time they had made friends with the office girls, and empty shell cases were handed out to everyone as though they were sweets. Most of the cases were eventually turned into cigarette lighters, whilst the airfield police rushed around trying to recover all of the live ammo handed out to all and sundry.

The bomb disposal crew arrived to de-bomb the airplanes. Frankly I have never seen a task carried out so quickly in the minimum of time or fuss. Thick mats were placed under each aircraft, the bomb doors were opened, the bombs safetied and they just dropped the babies onto each other.'

After re-fuelling, the two bombers took off again later the same day, and returned belatedly to Bassingbourn, where they were stood down for repairs.

In the period after September's re-organization, events were moving into a critical phase for VIII Bomber Command. During the weeks that followed, a number of innovations were introduced in terms of equipment and procedure which would go some way to solving the problems encountered by VIII Bomber Command during 1942 and 1943. In many respects it can be said that the winter spanning '073's operational career from September 1943 to February 1944 was the crucial time when the future success or failure of the daylight air offensive, and ultimately of the invasion of Europe, was decided.

On this day also, VIII Bomber Command carried out trials on North Sea bombing ranges in which a formation's bomb release point was indicated by smoke markers dropped from a pathfinder B-17 of the 482nd Bomb Group from Alconbury. Their aircraft were fitted with the British-designed H2S radar system which made possible 'bombing through overcast'.

This was a further development of the procedure whereby all the aircraft in a squadron or group would release their bomb loads on the signal of the lead crew of the formation, with the lead bombardier steering his aircraft from the bombsight via the Automatic Flight Control Equipment. Lead crews were selected from among the most experienced pilots, navigators and bombardiers in each squadron, a fact that did not go unnoticed by the *Luftwaffe*; in due course on some of the following aircraft, highly-trained bombardiers could be replaced by so-called 'toggliers'. Eventually each bomb group would have a small number of pathfinder aircraft on its strength.

Impressed by the bombing patterns produced in the trials, Eaker ordered the 482nd Group to make its operational debut by leading an attack on the German port of Emden on 27th September, in the anticipation that its coastal location would give a distinct radar image. Two of the 482nd's H2S radar-equipped B-17s were stationed at Bassingbourn on the evening before the mission to act as pathfinders for the 91st who once again were to be the lead group flying at the head of First Air Division, as part of a force of 305 bombers. Brigadier General William M Gross, commanding officer of the 1st Combat Wing, travelled in the lead B-17 as force commander, together with a squadron leader from the 482nd Group; shortly after take-off the H2S set in this aircraft became defective, a reflection of their early unreliability. Nevertheless the remaining pathfinder aircraft ensured that bombing results of their wings were fair, in contrast to those attempting to bomb visually.

On the same day for the first time, waves of US fighters were able to escort the bombers all the way to the target and back, using their new pressurized 108 US gallon auxiliary fuel tanks, and in the process destroy twenty-one enemy aircraft. These simple disposable devices would soon prove to be the key which unlocked Germany's air defences.

CHAPTER EIGHT

OCTOBER

Eaker was keen to use the new weapon again, and on 2nd October, VIII Bomber Command was ordered to return to Emden. '073 was one of four aircraft of the 401st again led by Captain Lay in an elderly B-17 called '*Bad Egg*', one of the squadron's original aircraft, as part of a formation of sixteen from the 91st. The pilot of '073 was 1st Lt Charles R Phillips who was to fly her on three missions in the space of five weeks. On this occasion Lt Phillips' crew included a flight engineer from the 324th Squadron. Led by two radar pathfinders, 339 B-17s dropped 953 tons of general-purpose bombs on the port of Emden in the space of six minutes, although one of the pathfinders released its load too early causing many others to be dropped short of the target. Nevertheless bombing results were adequate, and flak was reported to be moderate and inaccurate. Five groups of drop-tank Thunderbolts provided escort and only two bombers failed to return, neither of them from the 91st.

The 401st Squadron released their mixed loads of bombs at 4.10pm from 22,000 feet. Their results were not observed because of the prevailing weather conditions. Enemy fighters were seen but did not press home their attacks on the 1st Wing. There were no casualties.

If '073's first three missions had been a relatively uneventful introduction to air warfare, that was all about to change with early October's missions seeing some of the fiercest air battles yet encountered. The *Luftwaffe* had now gathered more than one thousand fighters for the defence of the Reich, almost all of them stationed within the borders of

Germany. These fighters were being equipped with progressively heavier weapons such as 30-mm cannon and rockets of 21-cm calibre for the express purpose of destroying bomber formations. In addition, a network of landing-strips had been developed across Germany where fighters of any unit could land for re-fuelling and re-arming; in this way the whole of the available fighter force could migrate from their bases towards the course of the incoming bombers and intercept them on both the inward and return legs of their journey.

On 4th October, '073 was not required to participate when the 91st despatched seventeen bombers to Frankfurt out of a total of 361 airborne that day. On a disappointing day the formation leaders found themselves 100 miles off course in poor weather; few aircraft were able to bomb their primary targets. Fighter opposition was fierce; altogether sixteen bombers were lost, and it was reported that losses would have been much higher were it not for the strong Thunderbolt escort.

Four days later, on the 8th October, at the start of VIII Bomber Command's most costly period of losses, '073 took part in her fourth mission. The First and Third Divisions were both despatched to attack targets in the north German port of Bremen, but approaching from different directions in order to split the fighter defences, while the Second Division carried out a diversionary attack on the U-boat yards at Vegesack. Although cloud and smoke in the area caused many aircraft to attack targets of opportunity, over 300 B-17s released more than 459 tons of bombs there between 3.05 and 3.27pm.

Bremen was renowned for the intensity of its flak defences; two-thirds of all the aircraft which passed over the target area received some degree of flak damage despite the first use by some aircraft of the Third Division of a radio counter measure codenamed '*Carpet*' designed to jam enemy gun-laying radar. Of the sixteen bombers in the 91st Bomb Group formation all but one were damaged, including '073, which was hit in the nose shattering the windows. The bombardier Lt Thomas W Kenefick was wounded in the wrist, above the right eye and in his left eye by flying glass; '073 had been blooded for the first time. Five of the aircraft were from the 401st under the leadership of Captain Eugene M Lockhart in '*The Shamrock Special*'. '073 was again piloted by Lt Phillips, with a mostly unchanged crew. The others in the formation were '*Bomb Boogie's Revenge*' on her first mission flown by Lt Pitts, '*Hell's Belle*' flown by Lt Evers and also '*Ramblin' Wreck*'.

The First and Third Divisions benefitted from the escort of the six available Thunderbolt groups. Nevertheless, as soon as the escort reached the limit of their range and were forced to withdraw, the *Luftwaffe* fighters appeared and began their usual pattern of attacks on the leading formations. The 1st Wing was again leading the First Division and, in a repetition of the events of the momentous Schweinfurt raid, the 381st Group flying in the vulnerable low position lost seven out of their eighteen aircraft, including the lead aircraft. In the 91st, one aircraft from the 323rd Squadron was attacked by fighters on the approach to the target and went down in flames. It was the same story at the head of the Third Division where the 100th Group lost seven out of nineteen aircraft.

In the 401st Squadron 'The Shamrock Special' and 'Ramblin' Wreck' were forced to abort their attacks; the other three aircraft released their loads of 500-lb bombs from 24,000 feet just after 3pm. Once again the strikes were unobserved, but the crews believed they had fallen in the target area. The Squadron diary confirms that anti-aircraft fire was accurate and intense over the target. It also records that 'Lt C S Hudson did a terrific job of first aid on Kerr and Youker'. These two sergeants were gunners in Lt Evers' crew, aboard 'Hell's Belle'. Both had been injured during the mission, Kerr almost falling out of his damaged ball turret door in the process, saved only by his safety strap. Charles Hudson was a former boxer who would eventually be promoted to Major as the 91st Group's lead bombardier; although this was only his third mission, it was the second occasion on which he had been cited for bravery in saving his crewmates, despite himself being wounded in the face by splinters.

On their return to Bassingbourn the three wounded men were hospitalized, and the ground crews set about repairing the damaged aircraft, patching holes in the aluminium skin and replacing smashed perspex. Of the five 401st aircraft despatched on the 8th, only two could be made ready for the following day. At their dispersal, Bert Pierce and his team were busy preparing '073 for her severest test so far.

The mission of 9th October, has entered the history of the 91st Bomb Group as its greatest air battle of the war. In the Eighth Air Force's longest mission to date, 263 'long-range' bombers were despatched to attack the Fw 190 factory at Marienburg in the far east of Germany and the ports of Gdynia and Danzig (now Gdansk) in Poland. Unlike the Second and Third Divisions however, at this time most of the groups in the First were still largely equipped with shorter-ranged B-17Fs. The 91st had been the last group to start receiving the new B-17G, their first five examples arriving only towards the end of September.

The 41st and 1st Wings were therefore briefed to fly a shorter mission to the Arado aircraft components factory at Anklam, on the Baltic coast, where Fw 190 wings and tails were assembled, in order to act as a diversion for the larger force further to the east. Even so, the attack on this nearer target would entail a flight of some 1,200 miles and eight hours duration, taking the bombers far beyond the distance of previous attacks and the range of fighter escort. This day's mission was the subject of the USAAF Motion Picture Unit's documentary film entitled '*Target for Today*' which went on general release for cinema audiences in 1944.

The 91st despatched a formation of seventeen aircraft led by Major Don Sheeler, commander of the 322nd Squadron, of which five were flown by crews from the 401st. In addition to the newly-repaired '*Lightning Strikes*' and '*Ramblin' Wreck*', the 401st formation included '*Buccaneer*' flown by Lt Pitts, '*Sir Baboon McGoon*' flown by Lt Phillips, and '*Tennessee Toddy*', one of only two B-17Gs so far allocated to the 401st. This aircraft had arrived two weeks earlier on 26th September and would be shot down on the following day, 10th October; this in itself was not unusual, several aircraft at Bassingbourn surviving for less than a week. Due to the extreme range of the mission the B-17Fs had been fitted with auxiliary bomb-bay fuel tanks, each containing 410 US gallons, which were to be jettisoned en route.

After an 0730 take-off and assembling their formation, the route took the 115 B-17s of the Anklam force out over the North Sea, at a height of only 1,000 feet to delay detection by enemy radar, across Denmark and then south east over the Baltic to Germany, eventually climbing to a bombing height of 12,500 feet.

This time '073 was being flown by Lt Evers' crew, and occupied the rearmost position in the low squadron of the 91st formation. Prior to entering German controlled airspace, a number of aircraft began to abort the mission, four of them from the 91st Group, leaving only '073 and the reliable '*Ramblin' Wreck*' remaining of the 401st Squadron. With the contents of the bomb-bay tanks consumed, the time came to jettison them. Aboard '073, as on some other aircraft, the tank was reluctant to drop; the bombardier Lt Hudson made his way back onto the narrow catwalk across the open bomb-bay and helped it on its way with a hefty kick.

Enemy fighters were first seen at the coast of Denmark and their attacks intensified as the force flew south-east towards the target area. The Anklam force was certainly serving its purpose as a decoy for the enemy; visibility was unlimited and substantial numbers of fighters of all types began to intercept. In the already depleted 91st Group, the crews watched the *Luftwaffe* fighters apprehensively, and concentrated on holding their formation; initially the attacks were directed at the leading 322nd Squadron.

The first Fortress to go down was '*Chief Sly III*' from the second element of the 322nd, flown by Lt Pinning, which was shot out of the formation by heavy fighter attacks just after 1100 hrs and crashed into the sea between Denmark and Sweden; all ten crew members perished.

Just before the formation reached its Initial Point at Neubrandenburg where the groups spread out into line astern formation and turned onto their bomb run towards Anklam, another aircraft from the 322nd took a head-on attack from an Fw 190 and dropped out with its engines on fire.

On the approach to the target, '073 was hit in two of her engines; the starboard outer started to smoke and had to be shut down to prevent fire. At 11.44am Lt Hudson released his load of 1,000-lb GPs and incendiaries over Anklam, the only 401st bombardier to do so. Anti-aircraft fire was coming up from the target and while '073's bomb-bay was open a flakburst smashed into her hydraulic system, leaving the bomb-doors without power. The crew of '*Ramblin' Wreck*' were unable to release their bombs at the target and were obliged to jettison them a minute or so later.

Usually *Luftwaffe* fighters kept clear of the bomber's target area to avoid falling victim to their own flak, but in this instance they continued to press home their attacks regardless. In the nose of '073, Lt Hudson and the navigator Lt Bruce Moore were in continuous action with their machine guns, snapping off bursts of fire at the oncoming fighters. Suddenly splinters from another flakburst came tearing through the nose. Hudson was knocked to the floor, his left wrist broken. Picking himself up and tucking his left arm inside his life jacket, he resumed firing with his right.

On the route out three more 91st Fortresses were shot down – a third from the 322nd Squadron, and two from the 323rd. Due to the number of gaps opening up in the formation Lt Evers was able to move up and formate alongside Major Sheeler's aircraft.

The fighter attacks continued all the way back to the North Sea. Hudson had been wounded twice more by flak splinters in both arms and had a sizeable hole through his right hand from 20-mm cannon fire, but he continued to man his gun. Between them, he and Lt Moore had used up hundreds of rounds of ammunition; Moore went back to the radio compartment to fetch a further supply, the belt being passed across the bomb-bay, through the cockpit and down into the nose.

'073's starboard inner (No. 3) engine was now losing power and once out over the North Sea Lt Evers found that even at maximum throttle he could no longer keep up with the formation and began to let down to a lower altitude. It had become crucial to reduce their drag; leaving the controls of '073 in the hands of his co-pilot, Evers went back to the bomb-bay and, sitting astride the catwalk, he hand-cranked the bomb-doors up into their closed position.

By now '073 was flying just above the wavetops of the North Sea and Evers ordered all removable items including the guns to be thrown out to lighten the load. Soon the ailing No. 3 engine packed up completely but Evers managed to coax '073 back to England on the remaining two. Eight and a half hours after take-off, '073 returned to Bassingbourn. Calling up 'Swordfish' – Bassingbourn's control tower – for clearance and firing red flares to indicate that there were wounded on board, Evers took '073 in for a two-engined landing. In keeping with standard procedure, he put her down on the grass alongside the main runway so that should a crash-landing occur, the runway would remain open.

This was just as well, for on touching down, the starboard landing gear collapsed, causing the aircraft to veer to the right and perform a ground-loop. In any case, the brakes were out of action due to the damaged hydraulics, but '073 came to a halt without further injury.

'Bud' Evers later summarized the mission of 9th October, in the following laconic terms:

> *'Anklam, Germany was the target thirty to fifty miles north of Berlin by way of the North Sea and Denmark. There were only twelve planes in the formation due to aborts. We flew in the low squadron as tail end charlie. Only four ships in the low squadron. An estimated 300 EA attacked for approximately four hours. We lost five planes. The bombing was accurate. After the target we pulled up on the left wing of the lead plane. It was a German turkey shoot. Our plane was credited with three enemy fighters. Our crew shot up nine extra boxes of ammunition. We had*

one casualty. Our bomb-bay door would not close after the target and No. 3 engine was smoking. We left the formation and returned to Bassingbourn on two engines. We were attacked from the Danish Coast going in to the sea going out by waves of Fw 190, Me 109/110, Ju 88/87 and Do 217. We departed the formation near Denmark at sea and set a course for Bassingbourn. The mission was about eight hours 30 minutes'.

For his actions on that day, Lt Charles Hudson was awarded the Distinguished Service Cross, as was Lt Sidney Hantman, the severely wounded observer/tail gunner in Major Sheeler's lead crew. The squadron diary records that up to 300 enemy fighters had been encountered; despite this, the bombing had been accurate with hits being observed in the target area, and the returning crews reporting dust and flames rising to a great height. The best bombing of the day was achieved by the Marienburg force, however. In the absence of anti-aircraft fire, they succeeded in placing eighty-three percent of their bombs within 2,000 feet of the aiming point; the factory which had hitherto been producing fifty percent of the *Luftwaffe's* Fw 190s was devastated.

Back at Bassingbourn it was obvious to the ground crews that '073 was going to be out of action for some time. The extent of the damage was clearly beyond the scope of Sgt Pierce's team. Later that day, '073 was jacked up to a level attitude and carefully towed to the hangar for repairs by the base Sub-Depot. In the event '073 was fitted with replacement wing and tail sections, two new engines and an undercarriage leg, and was out of service for the next ten days. Seven other Fortresses had also been damaged.

As a result, '073 was not available for the maximum effort mission to Munster on 10th October, when thirty B-17s were shot down, nor for the mission of 14th October, when VIII Bomber Command returned to Schweinfurt to complete the destruction of the ball-bearing plants which they had begun on 17th August. On a day which became known as 'Black Thursday', VIII Bomber Command suffered a repetition of the losses sustained on their first visit there, a further sixty Fortresses being shot down, forty-five of them from the First Division in its heaviest day of losses. A further seventeen were either destroyed in crash landings on their return or were later assessed as unrepairable, and 121 received some degree of damage.

In the four missions of mid-October, VIII Bomber Command had lost 148 bombers. Almost one and a half thousand aircrew members had been killed or taken prisoner. On the second Schweinfurt mission, losses had reached a staggering nineteen percent – way beyond the level regarded as prohibitive. Morale on the bomber bases had reached an all-time low; at this time B-17 crews were suffering a higher loss rate than any other arm of the US Forces. It was clear that VIII Bomber Command's offensive had reached a critical point. Despite the issue of press releases extolling the bombing results being achieved and proclaiming over-optimistic estimates of the numbers of German fighters being destroyed, it was apparent that the situation could not be allowed to continue. Although the bombing was indeed inflicting significant damage on key German industries, the *Luftwaffe* fighters, by concentrating on the destruction of one formation at a time, were forcing VIII Bomber Command to pay far too high a price for their successes.

Bert Stiles had this to say about the importance of maintaining a good formation:

> *'From the day you start out in B-17s they tell you that formation-flying is the secret of coming back every time. The* Luftwaffe *is always looking for a mangy outfit that is strung out half-way across Germany.*
>
> *When the* Luftwaffe *lies low for a few days, the formations begin to loosen up and string out and take it easy, then one day the Fw 190s come moaning down out of the clouds and the whole low squadron blows up and the high squadron piles into the lead squadron, and three or four ships out of a whole group come home. After that some pretty fair formation is flown for a while'.*

There was by now ample evidence that the bombers' survival depended on the presence of long-range escort fighters; in effect, the USAAF concept of the self-defending bomber formation was finished. As the bomber groups counted their losses on the evening of 14th October, it became clear that the Eighth Air Force could ill afford to mount further deep-penetration missions into Germany until sufficient fighters were available to escort the bombers all the way to the target and back.

Over the following three days in a series of memos and statements Eaker, Arnold and Roosevelt sought to put the US losses into perspective for the American public. A major victory had been achieved at Schweinfurt, despite the losses; it was suspected that the *Luftwaffe* was about to collapse and this was not the time to ease off. For his part, Eaker again pleaded for the allocation of more longer-ranged fighters to his command – P-38 Lightnings and P-51 Mustangs, and for thousands of long-range drop-tanks.

In fact, these things were just around the corner, but not yet quite to hand. On 15th October, the day after the second Schweinfurt raid, the 55th Fighter Group became operational from Nuthampstead in Hertfordshire, the first P-38-equipped group to fly from the UK in almost a year. With drop-tanks the latest version, the P-38H, had a radius of action of some 450 miles. Better still, at about the same time rumours began to circulate that a Merlin-engined version of the North American P-51 Mustang in US markings had been seen at an Eighth Air Force supply base in Berkshire; the new Mustang's reputation as the most capable fighter yet produced by the Allies had already preceded it.

For the time being however, VIII Bomber Command's operations were severely curtailed by poor weather. Only one further mission was flown during the rest of October; this was on 20th when, after a previous cancellation, 212 B-17s set out to attack aircraft industrial targets at Duren, just inside Germany. '073, by now returned to service, was one of only three aircraft despatched by the 401st, the only squadron of the 91st to take part, along with '*Bomb Boogies' Revenge*' and '*Hell's Belle*'. Before the force had entered enemy airspace the ball turret gunner in '073, Sgt Chester R Zimmerman, was taken ill and the pilot Lt Kenneth B Rutledge (previously the co-pilot in Lt Pitts' crew) and his co-pilot Lt William B McAdams were obliged to break formation and make an early return to Bassingbourn.

In the event, despite being guided by the 813th Squadron of the 482nd Bomb Group using the *Oboe* blind-bombing system for the first time, less than half the force were able to release their bombs anywhere near the target. Due to a failure of the pathfinding equipment, the entire First Division, including the rest of the 401st, aborted their attack on what their diary simply described as a 'poor day for the squadron'.

CHAPTER NINE

NOVEMBER

For '073, as well as for VIII Bomber Command as a whole, this was the beginning of a new phase of operations. No longer a new aeroplane with her patched and repaired sections, '073 was about to take part in a three month series of missions culminating in the execution of Operation '*Argument*'. The plan for this operation, the existence of which was disclosed to senior Eighth Air Force officers on 4th November, was for an all-out assault on the German aircraft industry at a time yet to be specified. For the time being, the plan consisted only of official guidelines for continuing the policies already being pursued, but it provided the blueprint for a series of decisive blows, to be struck whenever the tactical conditions were right.

'073 was not required to take part in November 3rd's mission to the port of Wilhelmshaven. The mission was significant as being the first led by pathfinders equipped with American-made H2X guidance radar (codenamed '*Mickey*'), the first in which a force of over 500 bombers was despatched by VIII Bomber Command and also the first in which a heavy bomber group was able to put up a double formation – fifty B-17s of the 96th.

Losses in aircraft were now being replaced more quickly, and although the supply of trained aircrew continued to be slow, the number of available crews was steadily increasing. During October the nominal number of heavy bombers in each squadron had been raised from nine to twelve. Despite losing nine aircraft during the previous month, the 91st were able to supply twenty-four for the Wilhelmshaven mission. Sadly, despite the initial presence of a fighter escort, after they had reached their limit and turned for home this day saw the 91st lose a further three aircraft to enemy fighters, all of them from the 401st Squadron and all of them containing former crew members of '*Lightning Strikes*'. Lt 'Bud' Evers' crew were flying alongside them, as his top turret gunner Sgt Capron recorded:

'Today we went to Wilhelmshaven, Germany. The target was the naval docks and buildings. We were again low group 'Tail End Charlie'. We had beautiful escort of P-38's and P-47's. The 38s are wonderful, and had it not been for them we would not have made it back. We had about 200 enemy fighters hit our group and things were pretty hot for about an hour.

Gibbs, the tail gunner was hit in the left leg by a 30 cal. Look pretty bad. He got one fighter before they got him.

York, the ball turret gunner claimed an Fw 190 and an Me 109. I'm sure I hit one but didn't have time to check to make sure he went down.

Our squadron sent up only four crews on this one and we are the only one that got back. The three that were lost were Lt Pitts and crew who were on their last mission, Lt Rutledge and crew, and Lt McAdams and crew.

Enemy Aircraft – three confirmed, one probable.

Bomb Load – 10/500-lbs, four clusters incendiaries.

Time – 6hrs. 18min.

Of these three crews lost, only five men survived to become prisoners of war, three from Lt Pitts' crew in '*Bomb Boogie's Revenge*' and two from Lt Rutledge's crew; none of the pilots were amongst them.

Two other events of note took place on 4th November; the personnel of the 354th Fighter Group arrived in England by ship fresh from training in the United States. At Greenham Common in Berkshire they were introduced to the P-51B Mustang. Although they were a new group, the 354th had been chosen as the first unit in Europe to be equipped with the new long-range fighter, making their combat debut just over a month later. Known as the 'Pioneer Mustang Group' they were actually a unit of the US Ninth Air Force, which had been created to provide tactical support for the Allied invasion forces, but like other such fighter groups until mid-1944 their services were on loan to the Combined Bomber Offensive.

Also on 4th and 5th November, the officers and airmen who were to be the pivotal crew of '073 arrived at Bassingbourn, transferred from the strength of the 2900th Combat Crew Replacement Centre Group at Bovingdon, Hertfordshire. This crew were a typical group of wartime volunteers in their late teens and early twenties from all parts of the United States. They had enlisted in the Army Air Forces when their call-up papers arrived during the summer of the previous year, and reported for duty as instructed in the autumn. After basic training, and having passed the aircrew selection procedure, they entered upon further phases of training in their various trades; they came together for the first time at Ephrata Air Force Base in Washington State during the summer of 1943, a base devoted to the training of B-17 crews.

First the six enlisted men were detailed off together to form the basis of a crew, sharing bunkhouse accommodation. Later on they were joined by the four officers, products of the 90-day cadet training programme which turned recruits into pilots, co-pilots, navigators and bombardiers, and under the leadership of Lt William F Gibbons the long process of forging the ten men into a combat crew began.

2nd Lt Gibbons was from Tuckahoe, New York, and his co-pilot 2nd Lt Clyde C McCallum from Washington State. Although only a year or two older than the rest of the crew, navigator 2nd Lt Donald E Shea from Iowa was generally known as 'Pop'. The bombardier 2nd Lt Wendell C Quattlebaum hailed from Elk City, Oklahoma. The flight engineer/top turret gunner was Sgt John R Parsons who grew up on a small farm near Lafayette, Indiana. Radio operator Sgt William O Douponce, nicknamed 'Blimp', was from Bay City, Michigan. The waist gunners were Sgt Julius W Edwards from New Jersey and Sgt Clarence R Bateman, usually called 'Junior', from Oklahoma City. Tail gunner Sgt Paul M Goecke from Dayton, Ohio and ball turret gunner Sgt Julius R Ginsberg from the Bronx, New York City completed the crew.

They flew every day, practising take-offs and landings and bombing runs, perfecting the skills they had been taught. After three months they moved on to Geiger AFB at Spokane, Washington, from where they flew full practice missions over the surrounding states in formation with other crews, and attended gunnery refresher school. In

September, they were sent to Grand Island, Nebraska from where they collected a brand new B-17F and, after passing their 'Preparation for Overseas Movement' inspection, set out for the UK via the Northern Ferry Route, landing at Gander in Newfoundland en route. Their crossing was uneventful and October saw the crew temporarily billeted under canvas in Wales, where they attended 'theatre orientation' lectures designed to unravel some of the mysteries of the British way of life such as wartime rationing, the sterling currency and the subtleties of our supposedly common language, all of which could cause problems for newcomers to the UK. After ten days in Wales the crew were notified that they had been assigned to the 401st Squadron, 91st Bomb Group and departed by train for Royston, the nearest railway station to Bassingbourn.

The six enlisted men of the crew were accommodated in barracks block 'D', sharing a dormitory with the NCOs of several other crews; meanwhile the officers were assigned rooms in the former married quarters:

> *'I lived in what we called a 'pilot house'. We started off in the 'H' blocks and as our seniority progressed so we moved up to better accommodation. The pilots who had been living there, weren't there anymore – you know how that went. It meant we were closer to making it'.* – Lt Donald Freer, Pilot 322nd BS.

Once installed at the base, the crew attended a five-day course at the 91st Bomb Group's ground school, each member receiving training relevant to their crew position. In addition, every crew member who was expected to operate a machine-gun in combat, including the navigator and bombardier, underwent further training on the airfield's firing range, which entailed shooting at clay pigeons from the back of a moving six-by-six truck. After that it was yet more training, this time in the air, to ensure that the 'rookie crew' reached the required operational standard prior to their first mission.

While the Gibbons crew were unpacking their gear and finding their way around Bassingbourn, VIII Bomber Command were in action again. On 5th November, five *Oboe*-equipped pathfinders led 374 B-17s of the First and Third Divisions on a mission to attack the oil refinery and marshalling yards at Gelsenkirchen in Western Germany, escorted by 383 fighters. The 91st provided a full-strength formation of eighteen aircraft. A flight of three aircraft from the 401st took part with Captain Eugene M Lockhart in '*Bad Egg*' leading '073, again flown by Lt 'Bud' Evers, and '*Ramblin' Wreck*'. 323 aircraft succeeded in attacking the target unloading 739 tons of bombs on the area between 1.15 and 1.50 pm.

Large amounts of fire were seen although results were unknown due to a layer of haze and a smokescreen. Of the fifty-one aircraft which did not attack, '*Ramblin' Wreck*' aborted before entering enemy airspace, the crew therefore not being credited with the mission, and '*Bad Egg*' was obliged to jettison her bombs prior to the target. '073 was thus the only 401st aircraft to bomb, releasing her load of incendiary bombs from a reported 28,500 feet at 1.44 pm. Flak over the target was intense with eleven of the 91st's aircraft being damaged, but although a number of enemy fighters were seen near the target, no attacks were made, as '073's top turret gunner Sgt Capron recorded in his diary:

> '*Today we went to Gelsenkirchen, Germany. We were flying in the high group, number two ship in 'C' flight. From the IP to five minutes after the target we had very heavy flack. It was also very accurate so we climbed to 31,500 feet but still couldn't get out of it. There were fighters in the target area but due to the heavy flack we had no attacks. Some of the groups were jumped on the way out but they left us alone.*
>
> *The target was the town and we think we did a good job. We had numerous flack holes in our ship but still broke the jinks and came back with no one wounded.*
>
> *Bomb Load – Incendiaries*
> *Time – 6 hrs'.*

Lt Evers, the pilot of '073, has similar recollections of the mission:

> '*Gelsenkirchen, Germany was the target. Because of the heavy flak we attacked at 31,000 feet. We had over five minutes of heavy flak from the IP until after the target. This was our first mission that we came back with all engines turning and no crew member wounded. We lead the high squadron (C flight) (sic). Our ship had numerous flak holes in the ship. There were enemy aircraft in the area but they did not attack us'.*

In the two weeks following the Gelsenkirchen mission, the weather over Europe again worsened, hindering effective operational planning and resulting in a number of aborted missions.

On 7th November, only '073 and *'Hell's Belle'* from the 401st were among the eighteen aircraft sent by the 91st as part of the 1st Combat Wing's mission to attack an aircraft industry plant at Wesel. The day's operations were hampered by a ten-tenths undercast, and bombing could only be achieved with *Oboe* guidance, which again proved inconclusive, the loads of many bombers being scattered far and wide along the borders of Holland and Belgium. This was the first of two occasions on which '073 is recorded as flying with only three gunners in the rear fuselage. This could be done from time to time as the need arose; the radio operator was on hand to man one of the guns if required and the two waist gunners often had difficulty in fighting back to back within the confines of the fuselage. In any case, at some positions in the formation one or other of the gunners could not operate without the risk of firing into friendly aircraft. Incidents of damage inflicted by friendly fire were by no means unknown.

Out of the fifty-nine despatched, the two 401st aircraft and four others aborted the mission without bombing. Sometime after crossing the enemy coast but before reaching the target '073's No. 4 (starboard outer) engine began to malfunction. Unable to keep up with the rest of the group Lt Charles R Phillips weighed up the options and dropped out of the formation. He turned '073 around and, taking advantage of the cloud cover, returned safely to Bassingbourn. Lt Phillips' crew, flying in '073 for the third time, and Lt Millard H Jewett's crew in *'Hell's Belle'* were both credited with the mission, however.

The flak was described as 'meagre and inaccurate' at various points on the route. Fighter escort and support was reported to be so effective that only one enemy fighter was sighted. In particular, on this day the 78th Fighter Group from Duxford, near Cambridge had sufficient numbers of aircraft and pilots to provide two separate formations, known as 'A' and 'B' Groups, operating independently, each consisting of three squadrons of twelve Thunderbolts, thus becoming the first VIII Fighter Command unit to do so. Even if VIII Bomber Command's escalating offensive could not yet be sure to destroy its target on every mission flown, it now seemed that, as predicted, the increased range and numbers of their fighters escort were starting to bring a reduction in the bomber's loss rate.

On 16th November the gales and low cloud over England cleared sufficiently to allow VIII Bomber Command to launch a mission with a chance of bombing visually over Norway. The targets were the molybdenum mines at Knaben for 189 bombers of the First Division, and a generating plant in the Rjukan Valley for the Third. Intelligence had indicated that both of these installations were associated with the German radioactive 'heavy water' research project.

At the head of the twenty aircraft despatched by the 91st were four from the 401st. In the lead was '729 *'Buccaneer'* flown by the squadron's Operations Officer, Captain James H McPartlin. The others were '073 flown by Lt Jewett, '767 piloted by Lt Evers and '795 *'Skoal'* assigned to Lt Julius D C Anderson. This was the first time since September that the 91st had been able to despatch more than the minimum 18-ship formation. The group leader Major Clyde G Gillespie was riding as Capt. McPartlin's co-pilot and, as was customary, a lieutenant was travelling as his tail gunner to report on the condition of the following formation. On this occasion the bombardier in Lt Jewett's crew aboard '073 was Captain J W Maupin seconded from the 401st Bomb Group at Deenethorpe. This unit had arrived in the UK at the beginning of the month, and would fly its first mission on the 26th, the first of a number of new units which would raise the combined strength of the First and Third Divisions to twenty B-17 groups by the end of the year. In the meantime, as was usual, its Group and Squadron COs and lead bombardiers and navigators were taking 'buddy rides' – flying missions as crew members with other established groups in order to gain combat experience.

Unescorted by fighters and untroubled by flak, after a long flight of almost 700 miles the First Division formations passed over their target between 11.33 am and 12.38 pm at a height of 15,000 feet, 130 bombers releasing 313 tons of 500-lb bombs. Unfortunately this was yet another abortive sortie for the 91st who, despite making two runs over the area, were unable to identify the target and eventually jettisoned their bombs into the sea. Four 91st aircraft were damaged but none were lost, and two enemy aircraft were claimed as destroyed, one of which was witnessed by T/Sgt Capron:

> *'Today we went to Knaben, Norway. We were flying in the low group as usual. The target was a molybdenum mine. The weather was so bad and the country was*

so rough that we never did find our target. There were no land marks of any kind and it all looks the same from the air.

We saw four fighters but only two made attacks. One made one pass at the formation and then left, and the other made two passes and was shot down. The pilot got out but he had a long rough walk home. The only flack we saw was ahead and behind us. We dropped our bombs in the North Sea to get rid of the weight.

Our altitude was 12,000 feet and the temperature -40 deg. C. We had no trouble to speak of and the only damage was two dents from empty shell cases.

Time – 8hrs.'

After the Norway mission the weather closed in again, and it was a further ten days before the next major mission could be mounted. On 25th November, the 401st Squadron diary records that Bassingbourn celebrated with a 'real nice Thanksgiving Day Dinner' followed by a party for the enlisted men in the evening at the Red Cross Aero Club with music provided by the base orchestra, and 'WAAF, Civilian and Land Army girls as guests'.

But it was back to business as usual on the following day, the 26th, when the 91st went to Bremen for the fourth time, as part of the largest force so far despatched by VIII Bomber Command. Of the 633 bombers taking off that day, 505 were briefed to attack the port area of the city. The 91st put up twenty-nine aircraft of which eight were from the 401st Squadron.

Of the 91st Group, ten aircraft aborted the mission before reaching the target, the majority as a result of mechanical malfunctions, including *'Buccaneer'* and '767 from the 401st, both of which dropped out of the formation before crossing the enemy coast. This time '073 had been assigned to the crew of 2nd Lt Julius D C Anderson, previously co-pilot to Lt Jewett, who were to fly her on five further missions.

After a dawn take-off, 440 bombers were guided to the target by pathfinders in conditions of extreme cold and icing, and released 1,200 tons of 500-lb GP and incendiary bombs between 11.45 am and 12.28 pm. Once again the results could not be observed due to cloud and smoke over the target.

The escort given by eight fighter groups was very effective, achieving thirty-four kills, the highest number of German aircraft yet destroyed in a single day and although up to 100 enemy fighters were seen, no attacks were made on the 91st Group. Altogether, however, twenty-nine Fortresses were lost on this day, and an intense flak barrage was encountered over the target which damaged more then half of the remaining 91st formation including '073. Another of the aircraft hit was '795 'Skoal', flown by Lt Tibbetts, who was unable to reach England and ditched her in the North Sea off Great Yarmouth. All the crew were picked up by Air-Sea Rescue and later returned unharmed to Bassingbourn.

For one crew however this was a day they would never forget. After three weeks of squadron training, Lt Bill Gibbons' crew had been cleared for their first mission, flying in the old favourite '679 'Ramblin' Wreck'. Sgt John R Parsons, then aged twenty-one, remembered it thus in his excellent memoir entitled 'The Best Seat in the House', a reference to his crew position of top turret gunner:

> 'We finally saw our crew on the 'Alert List'. This listed Gibbons and all of his crew members by name, and was posted on the downstairs hallway bulletin board. This list went up about 5.00pm and as you approached it, you could hear moans, sighs and groans.
>
> I had a sick feeling in my stomach whenever I saw our crew was flying. It sort of ruined your evening and it was even hard to write to Mai, as we could put nothing in our letters about our missions. All of our letters were censored. I thought that I was the only one with a deep feeling of fear. Later, I learned that you were not normal unless you were concerned that it could be the last day of your life. If we had flown two or three days in a row, and we had become very tired, it began to be more of a routine, our feelings later became duller. But the fear was always there. I reflected back over our extensive training period and thought to myself that facing death in combat was a time-frame in the future which could never be reached. In training, it was easy to doubt that you would actually have someone shooting at you.
>
> At 3.00am the following morning, the corporal woke me with a flashlight shining in my eyes, saying, 'Breakfast at 3.00, briefing at 4.00, stations at 5.15.' I learned to hate the hidden face behind the flashlight. I even began to hate the OD (olive drab) coloured GI flashlight and the 'Ever-Ready' batteries that energised that hateful light bulb.
>
> We shaved, showered and dressed. I always wore regular underwear, wool

underwear, and my wool OD pants and shirt. I had a thin pair of stockings, GI stockings and wool stockings. I also wore an OD wool sweater and scarf. Then my flying suit, electrified shoes (later plugged in on the airplane), and fleece-lined boots. I carried my silk gloves, regular gloves, electrified gloves and wool-lined leather gloves. After getting my helmet, I was ready to go out my barracks door.

After 'dressing', we went to the Mess Hall. Breakfast usually consisted of small Vienna sausages, powdered scrambled eggs, toast and coffee.

I picked up my parachute harness and headed to briefing. We sat on long benches facing a stage which was draped by a heavy black curtain. Briefing was a time of stress for the crews as you were being told where you might die, be seriously injured or disabled for life. I honestly do not believe that many men ever thought about becoming a Prisoner of War. The Commanding Officer would walk briskly down the aisle and ascend the stage. The CO would give us a pep talk, then turn the briefing over to the S-2 (intelligence) officer.

The intelligence officer would then slowly raise the curtain over the map of England and the continent. There was always a string of red yarn which started at our base and stopped at the German target. His devious habit of slowly raising the curtain would cause a low moan among the crews that rose into a crescendo as the yarn stopped at what we considered a rough target. The S-2 officer had marked the flak areas with red transparent plastic which he put on the map before the briefing. Then he would move some of them around so we got the impression he was not sure where the flak was located. His red yarn ran around areas that were thought to hold large concentrations. He could not predict where the mobile flak would be. The Germans had flat-bed rail cars which held 88mm anti-aircraft guns. He could predict with some accuracy where the fighter fields were located. However, he never knew just when they had sufficient fuel at any one of the fields, making it possible to engage the bomber stream and our fighter escort.

He always said, 'Don't worry, flak and fighters should be mild. This will be a good mission. Good luck. Jews go in this corner, Protestants in that corner, and Catholics in the other corner.'

The priest blessed us and gave us Communion.

We picked up our parachutes and our guns, and waited for a truck to take us to our airplanes. Usually the bombs and ammunition were already loaded.

The date was November 26, 1943. Our first mission was Bremen, Germany, which the veteran crews referred to as 'Little B.' Big 'B' was Berlin. We had been assigned to our plane, 42-29679, 'Ramblin' Wreck'.

All four squadrons had been dispersed to different areas of the field to protect them against enemy bombing and strafing. The bombers sat on hardstands connected to a taxi strip which led to the runways.

After the main briefing and the other specialized briefings, our crew met at the 401st Squadron hangar where our equipment room was located. It was here that we were to pick up our flying gear. The pilots preflighted the plane along with the ground crew chief and myself as flight engineer. We checked the exterior and interior of the plane to see that everything was ship-shape before takeoff.

When that was completed, we boarded the aircraft. The very first thing I did after boarding the aircraft was to check the bomb bay area and make sure that everything was secure there, to make sure that the bombs were fused as they should be. For some reason, I always had a fear about the incendiaries. They hung in the top area of the bomb bay and they were the first bombs loaded. I felt that they could easily come loose, but this never happened. Apparently they were secure, but I checked them each time. I had a habit of going to the back of the plane to see that everything was okay with the men. After that, I would go back to the front, place the guns in the mount, secure them and bring the ammunition up to the cover group of the machine gun. I made sure that the gun covers we carried them in were out of the way of any oxygen because they were soaked with oil. The first contact with oxygen would result in an explosion. I made sure the parachutes were lying in the proper place and checked with the co-pilot to make sure he had turned the dial for all the tanks.

I checked with the pilot and co-pilot as they went over their checklist and made sure that the procedure was followed. Once that was done, I felt comfortable in taking my position on the top turret deck. When the pilot started the aircraft, I made sure that there was no fire. We had a standby crew on the ground ready to extinguish any such fire.

It was necessary to make sure that the engine instruments were reading properly. When we received the call to move out onto the taxi way, I made sure that the tail wheel-lock was up, and then we started across the taxi way toward the tower.

I didn't put on my flak suit before we reached enemy territory. The armor plating and canvas in the suit weighed 20-pounds and was heavy and tiresome when wearing it at high altitude. I always wore my chest pack snapped on the right ring of my parachute harness. When I put the flak suit on, I risked exposing the right side of my chest area, but I felt the chest pack was thick enough to absorb low velocity flak and even some gunfire. Our suits were made of strips of magnesium steel sown in an overlapping fashion and extended from our neck to our groin in the front. In the back, it extended from about the lowest cervical vertebrae to an area slightly below lumbar vertebrae five and the sacral area, thus protecting must of the spine and interior vital organs. The suits proved highly effective as they saved many men from serious injury and death. We also carried a steel helmet that fit over our regular helmets. Ear flaps were designed to fit over our head set.

It was a beautiful sight to see all the airplanes in a line, each doing exactly as they were supposed to be doing. We sat in that position on the taxi way and watched for a green light on the other side of the runway. As we saw the green light, we moved up while the next airplane in position took off. Every thirty seconds, the green light flashed and an airplane took off down the runway, not knowing where the airplane was ahead of him, but knowing that by keeping the same rate of climb and speed, he would attain the proper position.

We would be going in over Bremen at an altitude of 28,000 feet. We had been told that we could expect very little flak and few fighters, which turned out to be incorrect. We were supposed to have an uneventful mission that day. We saw some spotty flak, but nothing to be concerned about until we made the turn. Then we got into a lot of flak. We were flying in the con trails and it was difficult to see where we were going. Over the target, I noticed that Tibbets was having trouble. He was our wing man and his tail seemed to be bobbing up and down. Then the plane disappeared. I mentioned this to Gibbons, but he was more of an optimist and assured me that Tibbets was right there somewhere in the con trails. I asked Gibbons to drop down so that we could look up. Sure enough, Tibbets had been hit bad by the flak and we learned that he had ditched in the Channel.

We came off the target and there were very few of our fighters around. However, one P-38 flew right along beside us out over the Channel. We would wave back and forth to each other. It was a nice moment.

Our crew was very tired and hungry. As we approached the base, our turn came to land, which was uneventful. Gibbons taxied the plane to our hardstand where we were picked up by a 6 x 6 truck. We were then driven to where we would be interrogated.

Our crew sat together at a separate table from the other crews. The S-2 (Intelligence Officer) came over and sat down. He asked a number of questions on what we saw in the air and in the target area. We soon learned that he had a set of questions all crews were asked. Since we had been in the air for almost nine hours, standing at that, the 8th Air Force had learned that the crews would open up more if they had a couple of stiff shots of Scotch Whisky with a small slice of gingerbread as an accompaniment. So he poured out a double shot and everyone drank them a bit faster than normal. This was to loosen our tongues. I'm sure that he received a lot of rapid-fire information after that drink. In fact, he tried to slow our conversation down a bit. At interrogation, the crews were always in a hurry to get back to the barracks, clean up, and eat. Some would go to town. But most were too tired and too stressed out to do anything but go to bed.'

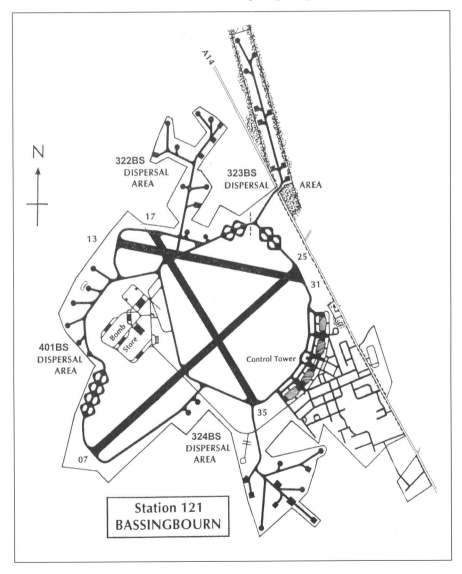

Arsenal of democracy: B-17F assembly line in full flow. (Boeing)

42-29536 'Mary Ruth – Memories of Mobile'. One of '073's predecessors as 'LL-A', assigned to crew chief M/Sgt Pierce, and the subject of newspaper articles by John Steinbeck, she completed six missions before failing to return from Huls on 22nd June, 1943.

42-3073 parked at Whitchurch airport on 23rd September, 1943 after returning from that morning's mission to Nantes. The second B-17 arriving is 42-29711 'LG-V' 'Chief Sly III' of 322nd Squadron. Also visible are a Hawker Hurricane and a Fairchild Argus. (Olmsted)

Cessna 152 G-BNSN after force-landing at Whitchurch on 10th November, 1993. (via author)

Butcher bird; the Focke-Wulf Fw 190 fighter (type A5/G3). Fast, agile and heavily armed, it was a formidable destroyer of Eighth Air Force bombers. (NASM)

A close-up of 42-3073 at Bassingbourn showing the arrangement of the nose-mounted .50 machine-gun. Note flak damage just forward of name. B-17 of 324th Squadron visible in the background. (Harlick)

View of 401st Squadron dispersals on the west side of Bassingbourn airfield on 15th October, 1943. Visible in front of '073 are an engine maintenance trestle, bomb-bay fuel tank and a ground crew shack together with various items of equipment. To the right is 42-5729 'Buccaneer'. Behind '073 is a B-17G; only two were assigned to the 401st at this date, 42-37742 'Vagabond Lady' and 42-39802. Both were shot down on 3rd November, 1943. (NASM)

Five B-17s of the 401st Squadron lined up on Bassingbourn's southern perimeter track in January 1944. Nearest the camera is 42-37958 'LL-G' 'Old Faithful', then 42-31187 'LL-F' 'Buckeye Boomerang'; 'Lightning Strikes' is believed to be third in line. 'Buckeye Boomerang' transferred to the group on 20th November and crashlanded at Deopham Green on 11th January on her return from Oschersleben. 'Old Faithful' arrived at Bassingbourn on 16th December, but crashed near Wincanton in Somerset on 25th June. (TRH Pictures)

Ready for take-off: more than twenty B-17s taxi towards Bassingbourn's main runway in early 1944; many have the natural metal finish which became usual from February onwards. Photo taken from the roof of 401st Squadron hangar. Also visible are a visiting Mustang and Thunderbolt, and an Airspeed Oxford assigned to the 91st BG for communications and training duties. (Harlick)

The Griesbach crew flew '073 in the opening mission of Operation 'Pointblank' on 11th January, 1944, and were her only crew to finish their combat tour together. L-R rear: John Hamner, John Piland, Roy Griesbach, John Simonson, Charles Peck, Ralph Rigaud. L-R front: Harry Small, Emil Viskocil, Robert Hartford, Harry Lane. (Griesbach)

The Weber crew who flew three missions with '073. All but one of the crew completed their combat tours on 42-31812 'Destiny's Child'; tail gunner John Paget baled out of 'The Liberty Run' near Leipzig on 20th July 1944. L-R rear: James Marshall, Louis Holland, Russell Ruth, John Paget, Eugene Letalien, Willis Kaltenbach. L-R front: Lt Moberg, James Fletcher, Donald Weiss, Howard Weber. (Paget)

Jack Bowen, waist gunner on '073, while on leave in London, late 1943. (Bowen)

Ground crew chief M/Sgt Bert J Pierce with his bride Inice on their wedding day. (Pierce)

Major *Heinz Bär (centre) and his wingman* Oberfeldwebel *Leo Schuhmacher inspect their 'kill' – 42-3040 'OR-Q' 'Miss Ouachita' of 323rd Squadron – at Bexten near Saltzbergen on 22nd February, 1944. Major Bär was the eighth highest scoring ace of all time with 220 victories from 1939 to 1945, and was himself shot down eighteen times. He was killed flying a light aircraft in 1957.*

41-24639 'The Careful Virgin', a veteran of 50 missions, flew with '073 on 5th December and 5th January. Despite her name, in November she demolished the tail section of 'The Shamrock Special' while landing with battle damage. '639 ended her days as a flying-bomb with the 388th Bomb Group assigned to Project 'Aphrodite'.

The last crew of 'Lightning Strikes', *pictured beside their aircraft, wearing a typical assortment of flying jackets, overalls, boots and headgear. L-R rear: Donald Shea, Clyde McCallum, Bill Gibbons, Wendell Quattlebaum. L-R front: Bill Douponce, Julius Edwards, Julius Ginsberg, Clarence Bateman, Paul Goecke, John Parsons. (Parsons)*

42-5729 'Buccaneer' *during take-off. This B-17 occupied the next hardstanding to* '073 *and flew with her on sixteen out of twenty-seven missions.* 'Buccaneer' *was returned to the USA in March 1944. (USAF).*

CHAPTER TEN

DECEMBER

Having received Category 'A' flak damage over Bremen, '073 was not available for the mission of 1st December in which five aircraft of the 91st were lost, including '*Hell's Belle*' from the 401st.

By 5th December, however, '073 was back in service in time for another significant day, both for her and for the Eighth Air Force.

On this day 548 bombers were despatched to attack several airfields and air depots in Occupied France. The 401st Squadron diary records '073 as being the lead ship of the 91st, at the head of the 1st Combat Wing, heading for the Renault works on the outskirts of Paris. At the controls was Capt. McPartlin with the mission leader Colonel Clemens K Wurzbach as his co-pilot, and Captain Slaton the group navigator; Lt Butler was riding in the tail turret as Formation Control Officer. Col Wurzbach had succeeded Col Wray as CO of the 91st Group in June, and had already piloted the lead ship of the First Wing on a number of occasions including the infamous Schweinfurt mission of 17th August.

Such was the current backlog of repair and maintenance, however, that only nine other crews of the 91st were flying behind Capt. McPartlin. Three of them were from the 401st – those of Lts Anderson, Phillips and Gibbons – but only one other 401st aircraft was airborne, '729 '*Buccaneer*'; two aircraft had been borrowed from other squadrons in the group, '*Duke of Paducah*' from the 324th Squadron being assigned to Lt Gibbons' crew and '*The Careful Virgin*' from the 323rd Squadron to Lt Anderson.

In addition, this was the day on which the 354th Fighter Group flew the

P-51 Mustang's first-ever bomber escort mission, from Boxted in Essex, under the leadership of Lt Colonel Don Blakeslee, seconded from the famous 4th Fighter Group.

Despite this auspicious start, the mission proved to be a complete failure. Two hours after crossing into French airspace, the formation returned with their bombloads intact having failed to find any sign of their targets through a solid overcast. No enemy air activity was encountered.

Capt. McPartlin recorded his impressions of the mission in his log book:

'The usual briefing, and Paris was the target. We took off at 8.15am with a thick fog rolling in on the field. It was my first trip with Colonel Wurzbach and also my first time to lead the Combat Wing. We climbed to 12,000 and assembled our group. The weather was good and all England below was just waiting for the dawn of a new day. Somehow I felt rather important and incorrigible to be leading such a large number of men and planes into battle. When the combat wing was assembled we left our departure point at the English coast and climbed to our bombing altitude 24,000. In perfect formation and like a great battle fleet we started across the English Channel to our target. In all directions one could see other large formations pressing on to their target. We crossed the French coast and I sent a warning on the intercom for all members to be on the alert. The enemy coast was visible but just beyond a cloud layer seemed to cover most of France in the vicinity of our target. We flew on course toward our target. The tail gunner reported flak below and to the left. We weaved slightly to make it more difficult for the gunners and in a moment we were out of the vicinity: the gunners reported fighters coming up from 6:00 low. The navigator replied that it was precisely time for our escort to arrive. They soon became visible and our protection was now on all sides of us, weaving in and out of our formation flashing a wing now and then so the nervous gunners could easily identify them. This was the first appearance of the new P-51 Mustang long range fighter and from my observation its had potentialities of a great fighter plane. The gunners did well and held their fire, because it does have a remarkable resemblance to the Me 109 German fighter. We continued on toward the target with solid overcast still below us. Our next rendezvous with fighters came very near the target. Almost at once the sky seemed filled with our old friends the P-47 Thunderbolts. A sight like this will never be equalled by anything a person can imagine, unless he is flying in a bomber over enemy territory. It can all be explained in two words. It spells Air Power. At times I felt we were a challenge for the enemy to come up after us. Finally we reached the IP (known as initial point)* *and the beginning of the bomb run. We could easily see our target was completely covered by cloud. We all felt very badly but the policy is not to bomb France indiscriminately. The trip home was uneventful. The escort fighters dashed about the sky looking for the Hun who was not there. The coast of jolly England looked good. It always does. Its a sight a person can't write on paper. It just beats in your chest but don't come out. We slowly let down from our terrific altitude and thankful to rid our countenance of the ever hateful oxygen mask. Once safely over land the gunners relax and jump out of their turrets and a constant chatter begins about the raid; everyone with his own comment. The combat wing dispersed and we start for home base. Soon the field appears and the majestic formations fly by as the ground grippers wait in awe. We check for landing instructions and soon we are rolling down the runway and then to dispersal area.'*

On her return from this mission '073 had in fact landed not at Bassingbourn, but some twenty-five miles to the east at Ridgewell, the home of the 91st's sister unit the 381st Bomb Group, who were currently enjoying a much better rate of serviceability. Unlike the 91st, the 381st had somehow managed to finish the month of November with all but one of their operational aircraft serviceable. It was therefore reasonable that Ridgewell's base Sub-Depot, the 448th, should take on some of the routine workload of Bassingbourn's overstretched ground crews. '073 remained at Ridgewell for maintenance until 10th December, when she was ferried back to Bassingbourn ready for the following day's mission. On 11th December, after several days of bad weather the 91st returned to Emden to attack the docks and industrial area as part of a pathfinder-guided force of 583 bombers. The 91st put up a full formation of twenty-four aircraft which contained six from the 401st – '*Buckeye Boomerang*', '*Jeannie Mare*', '*Ramblin' Wreck*', '073 and two unnamed B-17Gs – '*Buccaneer*' having aborted prior to crossing the enemy coast. The 91st formation attacked the target with incendiary bombs at 12.43pm, from a height of over four miles. Good results were observed with large fires being started both in the city and the dockyards. '*Jeannie Marie*' released her bombs almost half an hour later than the rest of the 401st Squadron after becoming separated from the formation and instead joining up with the forty-strong 351st Group, now part of the 92nd Combat Wing.

The scale of fighter opposition was varied; although the 401st crews reported a mere four single-engined fighters, of which only one Fw 190 made an attack, the leading sections of the force suffered sustained attacks by twin-engined German fighters firing rockets. In all, seventeen bombers were shot down, including that of the mission leader, in spite of what the crews described as 'effective support' by Thunderbolts, Lightnings and Mustangs.

Over the target the flak was intense and accurate, as John Parsons the top turret gunner on board '*Ramblin' Wreck*' later recalled:-

'All of the thirteen missions that I flew on were bad, but some were worse than others. There were a few that stood out in my mind. One of these was Emden Submarine Pens.

At briefing we were advised that there would be very little flak and no fighters. Our altitude was 28,000 feet. We had very little opposition enroute to the target area, but the target itself was like hell on earth. Flak was so heavy that we felt we could walk on it. The oil cooler was hit on the No. 3 engine and all the oil drained before we could feather the prop. We dropped our bombs and as we got out of the target area, we were swarmed by thirty German fighters. We dropped out of formation and proceeded to a lower altitude. Amazingly, there were no fighters at that altitude. We safely made our way back to Bassingbourn. The plane had holes all over it.'

In all, fourteen bombers of the 91st were damaged.

In the following two weeks VIII Bomber Command launched three consecutive attacks on the city of Bremen, the home of the Focke-Wulf 190 fighter – on 13th, 16th and 20th December. '073 took part in all three missions, as part of strong formations from the 91st, flown successively by the crews of Lieutenants Irvin Piacentini, Julius D C Anderson and William B Smith.

From the 401st Squadron's perspective all three missions followed a similar pattern – pathfinder-led bombing, often through overcast, in the middle of the day from heights of around five miles above the target, with the results being for the most part unobserved. The strong fighter escorts gave highly effective, if largely unseen, support with enemy fighter activity being severely curtailed, and relatively few bombers were lost. As usual, intense flak greeted the bombers over the target with a high proportion of them, including '073, being damaged. Although it seemed that the Americans might at last have the measure of the *Luftwaffe* fighters, there was still no protection from the flak.

Each of these three missions marked a further stage in the development of the Eighth Air Force's fighter operations. 13th December, saw the P-51 Mustangs of the 354th Fighter Group set a 480-mile record for the range of fighter penetration into enemy airspace, on their first extended escort mission.

On 16th December, the P-51 Mustang achieved its first confirmed victory over a *Luftwaffe* aircraft when 1st Lt Charles F Gumm Jr shot down an Me 109, and on 20th December, VIII Fighter Command's first so-called 'freelance' fighter mission occurred when due to high winds the bomber stream was thirty minutes late at their rendezvous with the P-38 Lightnings of the 55th Fighter Group. Taking advantage of the enforced delay, they ranged far ahead of the bombers to break up German fighter formations as they were assembling, a tactic which would later be formally adopted by the escort groups.

Also on that day was the first American use of a British invention known as 'Window' or 'Chaff' – thousands of strips of metal foil dropped from the bombers in order to swamp German radar with false returns, thereby acting as a 'smokescreen' for the bomber formations.

Although the 401st Squadron's serviceability status had improved since the start of the month, on the first two of these missions it was still necessary for aircraft to be borrowed from other squadrons in the group. On 13th December, Lt Col Gillespie led the group in *'Bad Egg'*, flown by Capt. McPartlin with a crew that included the Group Navigator, and a visiting Lieutenant Colonel as the tail gunner. Lt Bill Gibbons' crew were assigned *'Hell's Halo'* belonging to the 322nd Squadron, *'Ramblin' Wreck'* being unavailable due to damage caused by flak splinters on 11th December.

On 16th Demember, '073 was flying in formation with *'Quitchurbitchin'*, borrowed from the 324th, when she had a close shave as the top turret gunner Sgt Capron recorded in his log:

'Today we went to Bremen, Germany. The target was the centre of the city. Due to the ten tenths overcast we couldn't see the results, but are sure we didn't miss the whole town.

We were leading 'B' flight in the low group at an altitude of 25,000 feet. Some joker in the lead group got out of position and dropped a 500-lb bomb through our left wing. It gave us a few bad moments, but in spite of the big hole, we were able to hold our place in the formation.

We had fighter attacks going and coming. In the target area the flak was very heavy and accurate but we were not hit. Most of the fighter attacks were from the rear so we didn't have too much trouble there. The big hole in the wing was the only major damage. That guy Evers is the best pilot in any airforce.

Bomb load – 8500 lbs, 20 incendiaries.

Time – 7hrs, 20 mins.

PS This was my air medal mission.'

'We received an Air Medal for every five missions we flew. If a crew finished their tour of 25, they received the Distinguished Flying Cross (DFC). The Purple Heart was the third medal received by many airmen'. Sgt John R Parsons.

On the 20th December, after an anxious time climbing through thick cloud extending to 25,000 feet, it was Lt Evers' turn to lead the 401st formation in '*Bad Egg*'.

'Today for a change we went to Bremen, Germany. We were leading 'C' flight in the lead group. The target was again the centre of the town and today we had good visibility and very good results so we shouldn't have to go back there for a while. The entire eighth airforce hit the centre of the city and so there probably isn't much of Bremen left.

There were bandits in the area today but our wing didn't have any attacks. The flak more than made up for it, however, as it was as heavy as before but much more accurate. A Lt Col who went along for the ride was saved by a flak suit but Kerr the ball turret man was not so lucky. He was cut in the face by glass when a piece of flak hit his turret.

Our altitude over the target was 29,000 feet and the temperature was -55 deg. C.

Bomb load – 12,500-lbs.

Time – 7hrs, 25 mins.'

On their return, Lt Howard Weber's crew on their first mission managed to pull off a remarkable crashlanding at Marshall's Field near Cambridge after losing two engines to flak and running out of fuel, writing off 42-37767 in the process, while Lt William Smith, low on fuel, put '073 down on a vacant RAF base at Ludham, the first airfield he saw after crossing the coast of Norfolk.

On Christmas Eve the Eighth Air Force despatched the largest number of both bombers and fighters to date – 722 and 541 respectively – on the first of its so-called '*No-Ball*' missions to attack V-1 rocket launch sites in the Pas-de-Calais area of France, as part of Operation *'Crossbow'*.

2nd Lt Roy J Griesbach, whose crew had recently been assigned to the 91st, was flying as co-pilot in Lt 'Bud' Evers' crew to gain mission experience before piloting his own aircraft. Sgt Capron again:

> *'Today we went to Ardres, France. We were after the rocket guns the Germans have for use against England. We saw no fighters but the flak was deadly. We went over the target in nine ship squadron formation and due to this they were able to track individual airplanes with the flak guns.*
>
> *Our rudder controls were shot away and Sgt Young in the tail was hit in the leg. That makes six enlisted men that have been hit on our crew.*
>
> *When we landed our brakes went out and we tore up the ship trying to go through a barb wire fence. With no brakes and no rudder we almost wound up in the bomb dump. We tore off the left Hor. stab.* (tailplane) *when we just missed a concrete block house and then went through the barb wire fence. With 70 or 80 flak holes and the other damage the ship was a mess.*
>
> *I hope I never again see flak as accurate as it was today. There wasn't a ship in the group that wasn't damaged by flak.*
>
> *Bomb load – 16,300-lbs*
> *Altitude – 20,000 feet*
> *Time – 4 hrs, 15 mins.'*

Although '073 was still unavailable after the Bremen mission, Lt Bill Gibbons' crew were also taking part in this mission and had an equally rough time leading to the first change in their crew composition, as John Parsons later recalled:

> *'One of the worst missions occurred on Christmas Eve, 1943, at Bordeaux/ Calais, France. Everyone talked about it as though it was pretty much of a milk run. We flew at 18,000 feet and, again, flak was unbelievable. The shells burst right under the cockpit and filled the entire plane with smoke. The smell of gun powder smoke was overwhelming. We had lost track of our wing man. Another shell exploded in the nose section and hit Wendell Quattlebaum, our bombardier. I hurried to the nose section immediately. Wendy was lying face down. He was unconscious and covered with blood. I turned him over and took off his flak jacket and his oxygen mask. You could see that the right side of his face was shot up real bad. I administered first-aid by powdering that area with sulpha. Shea, the navigator, was backed up against the side of the plane like a scared rabbit. I kept*

shaking Wendy and he finally came to. He was dazed and confused and asked what had happened. At the same time he reached in his mouth and pulled out part of his jaw – teeth, gums and all. He mumbled, 'I got my Purple Heart.' I asked him if he wanted a cigarette and he said, 'Yes, John, please.' I lit a cigarette and put it between his lips. When he blew the smoke, it came out the side of his face.

We had dropped our bombs, so thank God, we only had to turn and head for home. I stayed in the nose beside Wendy the entire flight back.

Approaching the runway at Bassingbourn, we shot flares indicating we had a wounded man on board. Planes with wounded were allowed to come in first. As we were coming in, a plane flying under us crashed and exploded on the ground. As we landed, an ambulance pulled up to the plane and took Wendy to the hospital.

After looking at the plane, we all felt it was a miracle that we made it home. More and more, I felt that we had the best pilot in the Squadron'.

Altogether, eighty-five bombers were damaged, but none were lost.

VIII Bomber Command's final missions of the year came on 31st December, when a number of raids were carried out on airfields in Western France. Twenty-eight aircraft from the 91st attacked their secondary target, as part of a force of 296 Fortresses and Liberators, after bad weather had obscured the primary. '073 had again been allocated to Lt Anderson's crew. They were accompanied in the high squadron by eight other crews from the 401st, two of them flying aircraft borrowed from the 322nd Squadron. Capt. McPartlin was leading again in 'Hell's Halo' with the Group Operations Officer, Lt Col David G Alford, as his co-pilot.

On this as on other missions, the continuing disparity between the B-17F and G models is evident from the squadron records, with the two B-17Gs in the 401st formation, unencumbered by bomb-bay fuel tanks, each carrying forty-two M47 incendiary bombs, twice the bombload of the seven B-17Fs. In comparison to the recent series of missions to Germany – and with most of the route being over water – these raids were expected to be much easier. In fact they proved to be anything but a 'milk run' as Sgt Capron recorded:

'Today we went to Bordeaux, France. There was an overcast over this target so we hit the secondary target, an airfield at Cognac, France. This was a rough one today, and the longest one to date. We had some fighter attacks in the target area and some very accurate flak over the target and again as we came off the coast. We

had a number of flak holes in the ship but no major damage.'

Due to a strong fighter escort the 401st reported sighting only fifteen to twenty-five enemy fighters including, strangely, one Fw 190 in the markings of a Mustang. This was not the first time the *Luftwaffe* had been suspected of using various aircraft as decoys, as Sgt Parsons relates:

'I remember once, too, when we were coming out of southern France and we had one engine out. We were all alone. We looked down and coming out of the undercast was a B-17. It was different because it had the white star with the blue background, but it did not have the bars on the star. I told you guys that there was something fishy about this. Just keep your eye on that sucker. Well, it dawned on us that it was a spotter aircraft and that he was telling the fighter group where we were – direction, altitude, speed and so forth – and sure enough, here come two Me 109s. They went straight into the sun. We told everyone to just look into the sun, and at first sight of them, just shoot, man. Well, we didn't have to worry, no shot was fired from those people. When they turned out, they turned out on our left side and by God you could see those guys sitting there in their seats, those two pilots sitting there, they had on their white scarves. They gave us the wave off and went right down and blew that other sucker right out of the sky. Things like that happened, why were we so special to be complimented like that? It was just another lucky day, just another lucky thing that happened'.

Nevertheless, the bombers had to endure an intense flak barrage over Bordeaux; a total of twenty-five were lost, including two from the 324th Squadron, and another twenty-four aircraft of the 91st were damaged.

One of the 324th aircraft shot down, 42-29921, was flying alongside '073 in the 91st formation when it was hit, as witnessed by the top turret gunner.

'There was one plane I always liked – 'Oklahoma Okie'. It had the map of Oklahoma on it and just was a sharp paint job... a very colourful airplane. It flew along so well when we were in the same group. This particular day, these planes were off our wing, off our right side, and 'Oklahoma Okie' got hit. The pilot retired the engine somewhat and pulled off to his right, farther away from the formation. The plane was smoking really bad and the next thing you knew, a 20-mm round hit and blew the propeller over the airplane. The engine fell off and there is not a Goddamn thing you can do. You can grimace and grit your teeth or whatever, but there is nothing you can do. You are looking at a lifelong memory,

what happened there. I will never forget seeing that. You knew the airplane was going to blow up, there was a lot of smoke and then you see an orange burst come out of the airplane. When that happens, that is the end of it. The airplane was going down. I saw two chutes come out of the airplane. They no sooner cleared the aircraft than the plane exploded. Just blew all to hell. That's a terrible thing to see. Here you are tied to your airplane and you cannot leave your position because of the oxygen. You swear inside. You can do any damn thing that you want to, but you can't get out of your position. You have to stay there. And you just turn your head and go on.'

Five of 2nd Lt Bayard T G Dudley's crew in '921 were killed, four were taken prisoner and one evaded capture. Despite the flak, the bombing from over 18,000 feet produced good results with excellent concentration in the target area, where flames were still visible from the bombers twenty minutes after they had left the target. But as they set course for home, their difficulties were not yet over. After a pre-dawn take-off and an eight hour mission, the crews found themselves returning to England in gathering darkness and heavy cloud, many now short of fuel.

As night fell bombers were landing at airfields all along the coast of England from Dorset round to Lincolnshire. At least a further fifteen were either abandoned in the air or wrecked in crash landings, with more being written off through battle damage.

Lt 'Bud' Evers' crew aboard *Bad Egg* was one of those in difficulties. Having already landed once to refuel, they were unable to land at Bassingbourn and were diverted initially to Great Dunmow in Essex and then on to Andrews Field (Great Saling).

'As we neared the English coast we broke formation and headed for the nearest field. Reason – no fuel. We landed at an RAF night fighter field on the coast on one engine, the other three going out on the base leg. The fourth went out as we hit the runway.

Flying time – 9hrs, 5mins.

We refuelled and took off for home expecting to make it in about one hour. Soon after we took off the fog closed in and visibility dropped to zero. We flew over our field but couldn't see it. We then asked for directions to nearest cleared field and were told there were none. We did get a heading but couldn't find that field either. Finally with only 15 mins fuel supply left we found one that we could see from 18 feet off the ground. Visibility was still very poor and we swerved off the runway hitting a jeep, killing the boy in it. The left landing gear gave way and the plane was washed out. If we hadn't hit the jeep we would have landed safely. No one on our crew was hurt.

Total Flying Time – 11hrs, 35mins.'

Tragically, Corporal Gillies had been sent to put out flares to mark the runway for the incoming aircraft.

In retrospect, the final quarter of 1943 had been a disappointing time for the Eighth Air Force, with none of the strategic objectives of the Combined Bomber Offensive being achieved. There had been significant advances in terms of crews, equipment and tactics which boded well for the future, but most of the autumn's missions, although carried out with great determination, had been of little consequence. Few visual attacks had been made, the majority of raids only having been possible by means of radar guidance through the persistent overcast. VIII Bomber Command's worst enemies continued to be the weather, German fighters and flak, in that order. At the end of the year the Eighth possessed twenty-six operational bomb groups supported by twelve fighter groups, but still less than the number required to fulfil their planned objectives.

With effect from the New Year, there was a change in the status of VIII Bomber Command. Henceforth, in preparation for the coming invasion, it became part of the 'United States Strategic Air Forces in Europe' under Lt Gen. Spaatz with his headquarters at Bushy Park, Teddington, previously HQ Eighth Air Force. To mark the start of a new and more confident phase in its offensive, on 6th January, Lt General Eaker was succeeded as commander-in-chief of the Eighth Air Force by Lt General James H Doolittle from the Fifteenth Air Force in Italy.

Doolittle was an exceptional pilot and air leader, who had been awarded the Congressional Medal of Honor for leading a daring B-25 raid on Tokyo in 1942. His Air Corps service stretched back to 1918, and he had previously commanded the 4th Bombardment Wing in England in 1942. He understood as well as anyone that, despite the optimistic victory claims of the bomber gunners, it was only the long-range escort fighters which could eventually overcome the *Luftwaffe* fighters in the air and open up the skies over Europe for the Allies. But the fighters could not do so while they were tied to flying close escort on the bombers; their best results would come by going onto the offensive and working further out from the bombers, seeking out enemy fighters and using the bombers to draw the *Luftwaffe* up to fight.

Referring to the forthcoming invasions of Europe, General Arnold sent this New Year message to his commanders: 'Aircraft factories in this country are turning out large quantities of airplanes, engines and accessories. Our training establishments are operating twenty-four hours a day, seven days per week training crews. We are now furnishing fully all the aircraft and crews to take care of your attrition. It is a conceded fact that '*Overlord*' and '*Anvil*' will not be possible unless the German Air Force is destroyed. Therefore my personal message to you – this is a *must* – is to destroy the enemy air force wherever you find them, in the air, on the ground and in the factories'.

CHAPTER ELEVEN

JANUARY

The weather at the start of 1944 followed the pattern of the closing weeks of 1943, with fog and rain keeping the bombers on the ground until 4th January. On that day 569 bombers of all three Air Divisions, including the 91st Group, were despatched to attack the port of Kiel. After a difficult take-off and assembly in the pre-dawn darkness, 486 bombers succeeded in attacking the target, dropping 1,069 tons of bombs from five miles high through a ten-tenths undercast. The results were later reported to have been good, with heavy damage being inflicted on the docks area. Due to an effective fighter escort, few enemy fighters were encountered, but seventeen bombers were lost. Although all of the 91st aircraft returned safely, nine had been damaged by accurate flak over the target.

For this mission the 401st Squadron were obliged to borrow 'Miss Minookie' from the 323rd Squadron in order to make up their formation of six aircraft, assigning her to Lt Gibbons' crew. At the same time '073 was on loan to the 324th Squadron and was flown by 2nd Lt Uwell W McFarland's crew in a formation of seven aircraft, three of which were forced to abort, the first when 2nd Lt Allan A Uskela in 'Pistol Packin' Mama' was unable to find the formation during assembly, and two more with mechanical failures. Of the four aircraft remaining, '073 was the only one struck by flak, sustaining minor damage, but no casualties. Lt McFarland and his crew later reported seeing bomb bursts on both sides of the river in Kiel's dockyards.

On 5th January, the 91st took part in the last mission flown under the auspices of VIII Bomber Command, when 78 B-17s of the 1st and 94th Combat Wings attacked Tours airfield, escorted by two Thunderbolt groups, while other wings attacked various targets in France and Germany.

From this day the US Strategic Air Forces in Europe officially began to co-ordinate the operations of both the Eighth and Fifteenth Air Forces.

Coincidentally, this was also the day on which the 91st flew its 100th mission; as the first group in the 1st Wing of the First Division it was entirely appropriate that it should be the first unit of the Eighth Air Force to do so. As one of VIII Bomber Command's four 'pioneer' groups, this record had only been achieved at the cost of more aircraft and crews than any other group – ninety-one having been lost to date.

After another dangerous pre-dawn take-off, involving a number of collisions, to avoid the heavy weather forecast for the end of the day, the mission itself proved uneventful. Captain McPartlin was leading the 91st formation in '*The Careful Virgin*', borrowed from the 323rd Squadron, with the Group's new commanding officer, Colonel Claude E Putnam, as his co-pilot. Seven familiar aircraft of the 401st flew with him including '073, assigned to Lt Anderson for the fourth time. Each carried sixteen 300-lb bombs and the bombing results from around 20,000 feet were generally described as good, the target area being covered with bomb bursts and a high column of black smoke being observed. There was little interference from flak or fighters, although '073 was damaged by flak splinters for a seventh time, and crews saw a pair of rockets coming up from the ground to burst amongst the low group, one of the first occasions on which this form of air defence was reported.

The Thunderbolts escorted the bombers to the target and part of the way back; RAF Spitfires took over on the route back from near the coast to mid-Channel. Of the Tours force only one bomber was lost, that being from the 91st's sister group, the 381st.

Two days later, on 7th January, the entire available strength of the Eighth Air Force was despatched in cloudy conditions to attack the I G Farbenindustrie chemical works at Ludwigshafen – 502 bombers escorted by 571 fighters. After another difficult take-off and a number of aborts, 420 bombers succeeding in making a pathfinder-guided attack on the target with over 1,000 tons of bombs, the results being unobserved.

With a record number of fighters at its disposal, on this day VIII Fighter

Command for the first time employed the tactics of 'phased-escort', whereby, instead of being briefed to fly with a particular part of the bomber formation, each fighter group was allocated a section of the bombers' route to patrol while the bomber stream passed through it. Timing and navigation were the key to this technique in which the fighter groups took over from each other in relays at specific points along the route of the mission. This in turn allowed them to choose their most economical courses and fuel settings, thereby prolonging their available time with the bombers.

On this initial phased-escort mission the Thunderbolt groups patrolled the penetration and withdrawal sections in turn, with the longer-ranged Mustang and Lightning groups covering the areas around the target itself. The tactic proved so effective that it was henceforth adopted as standard procedure on deep-penetration missions for the rest of the war.

Five aircraft of the 401st were in the 91st formation – '073, again piloted by Lt Anderson, *'My Darling Also'*, *'Lackin' Shackin'*, *'Old Faithful'* and *'Ramblin' Wreck'*; the B-17Gs with sixteen 250-lb incendiaries, had twice the bombload of the F models which were required once again to carry bomb-bay fuel tanks. One other, *'Jeannie Marie'*, had been among the early returns. Interestingly in view of the new fighter tactics, the crews reported seeing large numbers of Lightning and Thunderbolts and also receiving excellent support from RAF Spitfires.

Up to fifty single-engined enemy fighters were seen by the 401st Squadron. Two waves of attacks were made, the first coming during a change over of escort from Lightnings to Thunderbolts. As usual the attacks were concentrated on the stragglers. Fw 190s were observed firing rockets at the formation and releasing aerial bombs attached to cables, but apparently without any real success. Eleven aircraft of the 91st were damaged but none were lost.

During the course of these attacks '073's top turret gunner Tech. Sgt Jewel C Maddox and tail gunner S/Sgt Aldrich A Seeley both scored hits on Me109s as they flashed through the bomber formation.

An elaborate system of checks existed to prevent the duplication of gunners' victory claims. Accurate assessment of the numbers of *Luftwaffe* fighters shot down was plagued with overlapping claims caused by numerous gunners engaging the same targets. For an enemy aircraft to be classed as 'Destroyed' it had to be seen to break up in mid-air, to go down enveloped in flames, or the pilot to bail out. Lesser degrees of damage would result in it being recorded as 'Probably Destroyed' or 'Damaged'. After de-briefing on their return to Bassingbourn, T/Sgt Maddox was officially credited with a 'Probable' and S/Sgt Seeley with one confirmed 'Destroyed'.

Altogether that day the Eighth Air Force approved claims for thirty-seven *Luftwaffe* fighters destroyed, thirty of those by bomber gunners. The pace of American production was now starting to overwhelm the German defenders; 8,000 warplanes were leaving US factories each month. During January the *Luftwaffe* lost 292 fighter pilots and thirty percent of their single-engine fighters. More seriously these losses were starting to erode the very fabric of its fighter arm; with every American attack the *Luftwaffe* was losing experienced pilots and unit commanders, who could now only be replaced by ill-trained youngsters.

By contrast, in the same month the number of heavy bomber crews available to the Eighth Air Force for the first time exceeded one thousand, with a similar number of fighter aircraft assigned.

On 11th January, '073 took part in her second great air battle, this being the third occasion on which the Eighth Air Force lost sixty bombers in a single day.

The raids in which the American bombers had all too often used radar to locate larger targets in the foul winter weather of 1943-44 were imprecise and amounted to little more than area bombing, quite contrary to the American vision of attacking precision strategic targets, but it was thought better to bomb inaccurately than to keep the bombers grounded.

Now, with cloud and heavy rain over England, but with a brief spell of clear weather predicted over central Germany, Doolittle seized the opportunity to send his force on the first 'maximum effort' deep penetration raid into Germany since October. In what was effectively the inaugural mission of Operation *'Pointblank'*, 663 bombers were despatched to attack five aircraft production plants in the region of Brunswick in central Germany. The objectives for the First Air Division were factories at Oschersleben and Halberstadt. Since the destruction of the plant at Marienburg on 9th October, the A G O factory at Oschersleben, the target for the six groups of the 41st, 94th and 1st Wings, had been the main production centre for the Focke-Wulf 190.

In anticipation of a deterioration in the weather later in the day, the mission was scheduled for an 8am take-off which would bring the bombers over their targets before noon and safely back to their airfields by 3pm.

The Oschersleben force consisting of 177 B-17s was briefed to be led by General Robert Travis with the 41st Wing, followed by the 94th, with the 1st Wing bringing up the rear.

The 91st Group was to lead the 1st Wing, with the 381st flying as the low group and, as had often happened before, the high group was to be a composite of 91st and 381st aircraft. This being a maximum effort, the 91st itself were scheduled to provide thirty-two aircraft – twenty for a full lead formation under wing leader Lt Col Theodore R Milton, plus twelve aircraft to make up the high composite group with nine aircraft from the 381st, led by Capt. McPartlin.

The planned fighter escort for the First Division consisted of a succession of two Thunderbolt groups en route to the target, the 354th 'Pioneer Mustang' Group taking over at the Initial Point, with two further Thunderbolt groups and six RAF Spitfire squadrons to cover the withdrawal.

With the 91st having suffered no losses on the three missions flown in the month so far, morale was good and the promise of Mustangs in the target area was reassuring. But the veterans of the Schweinfurt and Anklam missions knew how fierce the opposition could be in the skies over Germany; the *Luftwaffe* still had over 900 fighters stationed in Germany and Western Europe.

Of the ten 401st aircraft listed to fly, one – '*Old Faithful*' piloted by Lt Bob Tibbetts Jr – was not destined even to make it to take-off. While waiting in line on the perimeter track, '958 developed a flat tyre; Tibbetts tried to turn the aircraft out of the way and in so doing became hopelessly bogged down in mud at the side of the track, thereby obstructing a further six Fortresses behind him.

After much turning and dragging with tractors, thirty aircraft of the 91st became airborne and the Group and their Wing assembled without further difficulty, eventually departing the English coast over Lowestoft at 10 am.

It was over the North Sea that the plan first began to go awry; the cloudy conditions prevented the three wings of the Oschersleben force from forming into a single stream. As the sixty-one aircraft of the 1st Wing neared the Dutch coast at 10.30 am, it was noticed that 41st and 94th Wings had deviated to the south of their intended track to avoid some heavy cloud and were falling behind on their planned lead time ahead of the 1st Wing.

As the three wings headed eastwards at a speed of three miles a minute, the distance between the two diverging parts of the force steadily increased.

The *Luftwaffe* had been monitoring the progress of the bomber formations since their assembly over East Anglia, and planned to begin their defence just inside the Dutch/German border. More than 200 German fighters gathered on the bombers' route for what were to be the heaviest attacks since the great battles of the previous October. As yet there was little sign of the American escort fighters; soon after take-off they had entered cloud extending up to more than 20,000 feet, and several of the twelve Thunderbolt and Lightning groups had either aborted or failed to make their planned rendezvous with the bombers.

At 11 am the 1st Combat Wing found itself without escort when the *Luftwaffe* struck near Dummer Lake. As expected, most of the attacks were directed head-on against the leading formations with the 91st Group's lead and low squadrons and the 381st's Group high squadron being hit particularly hard.

At 11.38 am the 1st Wing were approaching the Initial Point when they saw the 41st and 94th Wings on a converging course from the south. There then followed several minutes of confusion during which the 1st Wing made their turn away from the IP, and the 41st and 94th carried out 'S' turns to come back on course. The net result of all this uncertain wheeling was that the Oschersleben force again formed into a single stream heading towards their target, but with the 1st Wing now leading and the 41st and 94th following. By doing this, they avoided the need to make one of the most dangerous manoeuvres in the book, that of a full 360 degree turn in the target area. As it was, the 351st Bomb Group at the tail end of the now reunited formation became detached in the turn and were obliged to bomb a nearby target of opportunity.

Even before the Initial Point was reached the 381st had lost eight B-17s to the fighters and the 91st, two, one from each of the 323rd and 324th Squadrons. The wing leader's aircraft '*Hell's Halo*' had also suffered heavy frontal damage; two of its engines were hit and cannon shells exploded in the nose, hitting the compass, bomb-sight mounting and radio. The bombers were now less than two minutes flying time from the target, and committed to a visual bomb run.

At that moment, at 11.45 am, faced with worsening weather, the shortage of escorts and the possibility that they might be unable to find their bases on their return, General Doolittle took the decision to recall the bombers. Whether this message was not intended for the First Division, or was not received, or was simply ignored, is unclear.

Whatever the reason, the First Division at Oschersleben and Halberstadt, and the leading 4th Wing of the Third Division at Waggum near Brunswick, were the only units to bomb. The first bombs to go down at Oschersleben were released by the 1st Wing at 11.47 am, followed very closely by those of the other two wings. Unfortunately the bombs of the 91st Group fell short of the target, landing on the town, their aim having been spoiled by the previous damage to the wing leader's bombsight; those of the 381st and composite groups, including the 401st Squadron, and the following wings, fell nearer to and directly on the target. Despite all the difficulties of the mission, much of the Fw 190 production plant was demolished, the strike photos showing the target well covered by bomb bursts.

In the 401st Squadron '073 was being flown by Roy Griesbach's crew on their fourth mission:

'I was indeed the pilot of the airplane on the momentous raid of January 11, 1944 on Oschersleben, Germany. I was flying in the No. 2 position in the lead squadron of the composite group.

The briefing before takeoff was notable in that when the curtain covering the large map with the flight path outlined with a heavy red string was swept open the initial approach to the target was straight on to Berlin (which had not yet been bombed in daylight). We stared at that line knowing that the enemy would be all-out for any attempt to bomb the capital and boded rough skies ahead. Then the line broke SW toward Oschersleben about ninety miles away.

Take off heavily laden with full bay tank, flak jackets, bombs – 21 x 130-lb incendiaries – ten crew required all the runway available. The skies were grey, ceiling very low and we were immediately on instruments in deep overcast. We climbed in a shallow left turn. After some time we started to break out into brilliant sunshine. We spotted the lead ship shooting red flares to facilitate its location for the rest of the assembly. Now we were able to breath more easily and slide into our assigned position in the group. At ten thousand we donned our oxygen masks. The gunners test fired their guns and stared ahead for the approach of the enemy coastline. Not known to us in the leading wing of the whole force, there was a recall and scrubbing of the whole mission. It was determined that with the deteriorating weather conditions getting all the planes on the ground was going to be hazardous.

So the two other wings turned back with the leading wing proceeding on to the target as briefed. This put us in a vastly reduced strength. With the line of flight directly toward Berlin the Germans would be on with overwhelming numbers. And so it would be. We did not know this but we would see shortly what the enemy was putting out for us. After turning from the Initial Point toward the bomb run my first indication of action was a call to tighten up the formation. At position ten o' clock high was at least a schwarm *(flight) of fighters pulling ahead and turning into formation firing head-on then diving straight down giving our gunners but a second or two for firing. Just before this I saw a flight of P-51s on our right just above us and streaking into the Germans. I believe that this flight of fighters was led by James Howard although I have not been able to prove this outright. Howard shot down six enemy planes on that one mission earning for him the Congressional Medal of Honor. On the bomb run the flak was accurate and heavy. I saw a B-17 explode just a bit behind us and lower. All was chaos. My navigator claimed one fighter shot down. My ball turret operator two. On my left I saw an Me 109 passing through the formation no farther than 200 feet with the pilot slumped over and his plane seemingly in a near stall. Turning off the target the flak slackened and the fighters continued pressing attacks all the way back to the coastline. This day our lost planes from this mission numbered five from our group and sixty for the whole attacking force that remained in the mission after the recall'.*

The German attacks continued as far as the target, and on the way back many of the massed fighters intercepted the bomber stream for a second time. Three more B-17s were lost from the 91st formation on the return journey, two from 322nd Squadron and Lt Uskela's crew in 'Little Jean' from 324th, bringing the total losses from the wing to thirteen.

The only friendly fighters to remain with the bombers all the way to the target and back were the forty-four Mustangs of the 354th Group. The presence of these aircraft over central Germany for the first time must have come as a shock for the *Luftwaffe*; although briefed to save their fire for the bombers, the German fighter pilots were no longer able to avoid combat with American fighters in their own skies. Despite being heavily outnumbered, the 354th Group fought magnificently destroying fifteen enemy aircraft for no loss to themselves.

On this day the commanding officer of the 356th Squadron in the 354th Fighter Group, Major James H Howard, did indeed win America's highest award for valour in a Mustang coded 'AJ-X' (his usual 'Ding Hao' being under repair) when, finding himself separated from the rest of his unit, he single-handedly defended the 401st Bomb Group B-17 formation in the 94th Wing against thirty German fighters over Halberstadt, shooting down at least three and damaging others. For twenty-five minutes, with his guns failing and his fuel running low, Howard continued to ward off German attacks and in so doing became the only fighter pilot to earn the Medal of Honor in Europe.

Elsewhere the top-scoring 56th Fighter Group, whose Thunderbolts had been modified in the previous few days with boosted engines, broad-bladed propellers and underwing drop-tanks, were engaged on the first official 'freelance' mission. Divided into two subgroups, 56'A' led by Lt Col Dave Schilling and 56'B' under Major Frank Gabreski, they ranged far ahead and to the sides of the bomber stream, destroying a further eleven fighters near Osnabruck. In all, the *Luftwaffe* lost thirty-nine aircraft.

Altogether, the aircraft of the First Division received more than 400 individual fighter attacks, and ground-to-air rockets were seen to release incendiary bombs which drifted through the formation on parachutes. The gunners of the 401st Squadron claimed a number of German fighters of all types destroyed and damaged.

For the Griesbach crew aboard '073, General Doolittle's misgivings proved to be well-founded:

'Over the North Sea we started the letdown and at 10,000 removed our oxygen masks and was able to relax somewhat. I reached for my candy bar that I had placed on the shelf on the top gun turret. Nothing ever tasted so good. Presently we received the word that the field was closed in and to take alternate fields. When we crossed over the English coastline we were down to a few hundred (feet) in heavy fog and overcast. When we reached the nearest field suggested the sky was filled with airplanes trying to land. Now my red lights came on indicating that we were running out of gas. We were flying lower and lower to keep the field in sight. Finally I got in the landing line-up for a chance at landing. On the approach I got the red light as two airplanes were on the runway and burning and I had to go around. Those red lights have been on and we are in trouble. We cannot land, we cannot climb to altitude, we are just above the tree tops. The planes are all calling in. The talk is jamming the air. We are going to be out of gas any minute now. What to do? I got a call from my navigator saying he 'thinks they have directed us to fly 175 degrees for six minutes for another field'. We take the heading and fly for

the six minutes. My co-pilot and I discuss this situation. No field. I call on the interphone and advise the crew that we will climb to 1,000 and bail out immediately at the sound of the alarm. Just as I am powering up off to my left, a long runway and a green light. We pull a fast landing check, wheels down, full flap, generators on, full rich mixture, high rpm and flop onto that beautiful runway. As we slow we see that the field is not finished and the sides of the runway are not yet filled in. As we turn now off the end of the runway onto the taxi strip No. 4 engine cuts out, out of gas. Did I mention that it had started to snow during all this? With the low frequency radios back then snow caused static and hearing was a problem.

Soon here we are now in the hardstand. The engines are cut, I can hear movement in the rear of the plane as the crew crawls out. I look at Charlie Peck, my co-pilot. What can be said? He looks exhausted, sweaty, and thoughtful. This is our fourth mission. We have twenty six more to go.

As for 'Lightning Strikes' No. 073, she performed very well. The details of this raid are seared into my brain. At the time one just hoped for an airplane that one is assigned to that it hasn't been abused in previous raids, either by battle damage or rough handling by the crews'.

In fact '073 had landed at Old Buckenham, the home of a Liberator group, south-west of Norwich. By the time the First Division returned to England the weather had already closed in and many aircraft were directed to alternative airfields in Norfolk and Suffolk. Only five crews of the 91st succeeded in finding their way through the overcast to Bassingbourn. The other twenty aircraft made landings at seven other bases nearer to the coast including Hethel and Deopham Green; at both of these bases a 91st Fortress – the lead ship 'Hell's Halo' and 'Spirit of '44' from the 322nd Squadron respectively – was written off due to combat damage.

These many diversions caused so much difficulty and confusion that it was decided that they would not be repeated in future unless absolutely necessary. 'Buckeye Boomerang' was so badly damaged when she slid off the end of the icy runway at Deopham Green that repairs were not completed until March. Although a number had sustained various degrees of damage, all the aircraft despatched by the 401st Squadron returned from the mission. In all, however, forty-two Fortresses of the First Division were missing in action, as were eighteen bombers from the Second and Third Divisions.

In recognition of their determination, the groups which had succeeded in reaching their targets were all later awarded a Distinguished Unit Citation. For the 91st this was their second battle honour, the Eighth Air

Force's first such distinction having been received for making the first American attack on the Ruhr industrial area, at the Hamm marshalling yards in the previous March.

In spite of its successes, the day was a salutary reminder that without an adequate escort along the entire route and favourable weather, deep penetrations into Germany were still too costly in aircrew and aircraft. The next stage in Operation '*Pointblank*' would have to be delayed until both of these conditions could be met.

In the days following the Oschersleben raid, persistent heavily clouded skies over Germany meant that only short-range missions and training flights over the UK could be attempted. Several operations were scheduled only to be scrubbed or recalled, with only two attacks on V-weapon sites in France being successfully accomplished. Towards the end of the month with so much time on their hands the aircrews were becoming bored and restless.

The monotony was broken on 23rd when the RAF's Enemy Aircraft Flight were at Bassingbourn with a trio of captured *Luftwaffe* types – a Ju 88, Me 109 and Me 110 – for recognition training purposes. After examining these aircraft on the ground, the 91st crews flew a practice mission with twenty-six B-17s while the two Messerschmitts carried out simulated attacks on their formation. Two days later, the *Luftwaffe* 'circus' continued on its tour of USAAF bases with an escort of Thunderbolts to ensure that it was not mistaken for the genuine article.

S/Sgt John 'Jack' Paget, aged twenty, the tail gunner in Lt Weber's crew, who had flown their second mission on 21st January, later recalled this period in his memoir '*Destiny's Child*':

> '*On January 24, 1944, we were on our way for a Frankfurt, Germany raid, and were recalled just after passing over the coastline into France, due to bad weather over the continent. Then, two days later, after briefing and all other preparations for a mission again scheduled for Frankfurt, it too did not materialize and was scrubbed due to the continuing bad weather. At least this time we did not get airborne. Scrubbed and recalled missions do not count so I was having trouble getting in that third mission, and also was being held on base and unable to get into Baldock to see my girl, Joan*'.

More than two weeks after the Oschersleben mission '073 was assigned to Lt Weber's crew as one of thirteen 401st Squadron aircraft led by Capt.

McPartlin when, at the third attempt, the record number of 863 bombers succeeding in reaching Frankfurt to attack the I G Farben chemical plant and the Varenigte Deutsche Metall works, escorted by 632 fighters. S/Sgt Paget again:

'January 29th, we were alerted for a mission to Frankfurt. We were scheduled to fly a B-17F, tail number 073. Today we carried twenty one 100-pound incendiary bombs and a bomb bay fuel tank. Take off was at 7.40 am and we climbed to 23,800 feet, temperatures reached minus thirty five degrees. Over 800 heavy bombers hit Frankfurt this day, the largest armada to date, and they showered 1,500 tons of bombs on this hapless city. Enemy fighters tried new tactics. Up to ten to twenty Focke-Wulfs and Messerschmitts made big concerted attacks against the big Fortresses, but our long range Mustang fighters did their job by chasing them away. As usual the flak was very heavy and again luckily we came away without damage. Time on oxygen was five hours and mission time lasted seven hours twenty five minutes. It was a long and tiring day. I now had three of my missions behind me'.

The target was covered by ten-tenths cloud and bombing was only achieved by the pathfinder technique. Twenty-nine bombers were shot down by flak or fighters; five more crash-landed in the UK or were written off, including the brand-new B-17G 42-37987 'Man O' War-Horsepower Ltd' from the 91st, irreparably damaged by German fighters on her first mission. However at least fifty-five German fighters had been destroyed or damaged in the day's actions.

On the following day, 30th January, Lt Weber's crew flew '073 for a second time, on their fourth mission. The 401st provided a basic squadron formation of six bombers as part of a force of 777 despatched in a further attack on aircraft industry targets in the Brunswick area, escorted by 635 fighters.

In the event, the mission developed into yet another pathfinder exercise when the primary targets could not be located visually through the undercast, and 703 bombers released over 1,200 tons of bombs on the industrial area of the city, the results being unobserved. The cloudy skies hampered the Germans as much as they did the thirteen American escort groups, but the 401st Squadron nevertheless encountered up to fifty enemy fighters and was subjected to two major attacks, the first on the approach to the target and the second near the German/Dutch border on the return leg.

Three crews of the 401st sustained casualties; '*My Darling Also*' and '*The Shamrock Special*' both returned with wounded gunners on board, while Lt Price brought '*Old Faithful*' back with his radio operator killed and his top turret gunner injured, both by enemy machine-gun fire. But the Americans had given a good account of themselves in the fight; the left waist gunner in '073, S/Sgt Eugene R Letalien, aged 24, claimed an Me 109 destroyed and an Fw 190 'probable', and six other crew members in the 401st were also credited with air-to-air victories.

As S/Sgt Paget later recalled:-

> '*As if our mission yesterday wasn't enough to hold us over for a day or two, it was not to be. The very next day our crew was alerted for another mission. During briefing the next morning we learned that our target was Brunswick, Germany. Brunswick lies 120 miles west of Berlin. Again we had the same plane as yesterday, the B-17F, number 073. But this time we were loaded with six 500 pound bombs and, of course, the bomb bay fuel tank. Temperatures again was minus thirty five degrees and altitude 23,000 feet. We took off at 7.20 am, climbing to altitude and forming our group and then headed for the continent of Europe. There were over 800 Fortresses and Liberators. We were on oxygen for five hours and fifteen minutes and the mission was eight hours and twenty minutes in duration. This time 1800 tons of bombs were unloaded over the target. We were attacked by the same enemy fighters, Fw 190s and Me 110s. Flak over the target was moderate. This time we had two holes in the leading edge of our left wing. No personal injuries to any of my crew members. I now had flown my fourth mission*'.

With twenty-two missions to her credit '073 was by now a comparatively elderly and battle-worn bomber. In early 1944 the average operational life expectancy of both an aircrew and a B-17 in the Eighth Air Force had risen to just twenty-one missions. It remained to be seen by how much '073 would exceed that figure.

CHAPTER TWELVE

FEBRUARY

The bad weather continued into the start of February, restricting the Eighth Air Force to the familiar pattern of pathfinder attacks through cloud on ports and cities in Germany, or short-range missions to targets in France when conditions allowed.

'073's next and penultimate series of missions were flown on 3rd, 4th and 6th February, and in a near-repetition of the three Bremen missions of mid-December, she was flown successively by the crews of Lieutenants Anderson, Smith and Piacentini.

On 3rd, the 401st Squadron again supplied six aircraft for a formation of 553 B-17s of the First and Third Divisions, which dropped 1,400 tons of bombs on the port of Wilhelmshaven from a height of 28,000 feet through a ten-tenths cloud layer. Alongside '073 were the familiar *'Buccaneer'*, *'The Shamrock Special'* and *'Lackin' Shackin'* and two newcomers, *'Corn State Terror'* recently transferred from the 324th Squadron, and *'Buckeye Boomerang II'*, a successor to the Fortress 42-31187 of the same name, flown by Lt James R Lutz.

At the post-mission debriefing, the crews unanimously praised the support given by their escort of 632 fighters, some saying that it was the best so far. So close and continuous was the cover that the 91st had encountered no enemy fighters at all, although nine of its aircraft were damaged by the accurate radar-directed flak which tracked them over the target. Only four bombers were lost this day, including two which collided over the North Sea. The fighters claimed eight German aircraft destroyed, the bombers none.

Aboard '073, Lt Anderson's crew was largely unchanged from December/January except where Sergeants Jack Bowen and Kenneth P Fiigen had been substituted in the waist gunner positions. Overall this was a routine mission, carried out with little difficulty, although the results were of course unobserved.

During the evening, after the bombers had returned to Bassingbourn, a field order began to come off the teleprinter in the group HQ requiring the 91st to find thirty-three airworthy bombers for another mission on the following day, 4th February, as S/Sgt Paget records:

> 'That night our crew's name came up on the alert board for a mission the next day. What else, another trip to Frankfurt as we looked at the red tape going in and the green one coming out on the big map in the briefing room. Along these tapes were the fighter silhouette locations where we could expect to pick up our escort. On this mission we had a newer aircraft, a B-17G with tail number of 929 (Lackin' Shackin'). Bomb load was twelve 500 pounders, because no bomb bay fuel tank was needed for this model. Altitude today would be very high at 26,000 feet.
>
> We took off at 7.25am, and after completing our formation at altitude, headed for the continent, soon crossing over the English Channel. From the tail looking back, I could see the White Cliffs of Dover, a magnificent sight for a young airman who has been launched into an amazing world that he had never realized existed.
>
> Even though the losses of twenty one bombers were reported as missing in the following days newspaper reports, our group was not encountered by enemy fighters again. Flak was however extremely heavy and accurate, and our aircraft sustained holes in the right waist and plexiglas nose, as well as between numbers 1 and 2 engines. Temperatures dipped to minus forty-five degrees Fahrenheit and we were on oxygen five hours and twenty-five minutes. The time in the air was seven hours and forty-five minutes. A long day.'

Despite the flak damage of the previous day, nine aircraft from the 401st took part in this mission, at least until '572 *My Beloved Too*' aborted with a supercharger out prior to entering enemy airspace. Once again the target was covered in cloud and of the 748 bombers despatched, only 373 succeeded in attacking their secondary target, the railway marshalling yards at Frankfurt, by the pathfinder method, while 160 more attacked other 'targets of opportunity' across north-west Germany. The fighter escort again provided good support and no enemy fighters were encountered. Anti-aircraft fire in the target area was moderate and inaccurate, but the bombers met an intense barrage over the Ruhr on the return journey. Altogether twenty bombers were lost, three of them from the 91st – the group leader Lt Col Alford in a pathfinder B-17 of the 482nd Bomb Group, '803 '*The Wolf*' of the 324th Squadron and '771 '*Jeannie Marie*' flown by Lt Lutz of the 401st. The manner of '*Jeannie Marie*'s passing was not known at the time; she was last seen near Antwerp where strong crosswinds blew the formation into an area of concentrated flak. A number of other aircraft in the group sustained considerable damage.

The 6th February's mission was an uneventful failure. The 401st supplied seven aircraft and nine crews of the 91st's thirty-three bombers in a force of 642 despatched to attack four *Luftwaffe* airfields in France. Having failed to locate their target at Nancy-Essey through six to eight-tenths undercast, or even to identify a target outline by radar, the 91st returned to base with their bombs, safe but disappointed.

Yet again no enemy fighters were seen, probably due to the presence of the P-51 escort, which was described as being 'especially good in the target area', and the flak was at worst moderate. Of the 303 aircraft in the First Air Division, only sixty succeeded in finding and bombing other airfields as targets of opportunity, but only one B-17 was lost to enemy action, although 42-40025 '*Touch the Button Nell*' of the 381st Group crashlanded at the US Navy's Liberator base at Dunkeswell in Devon on the route back where she was later written off.

The most significant aspect of the day's events, however, related not to the bombers, but to the 638 fighters escorting them. In carrying out General Arnold's New Year order to destroy the *Luftwaffe* wherever they could be found, VIII Fighter Command had already begun extending their freelance tactics to include the shooting up or 'strafing' of *Luftwaffe* airfields by fighters returning from bomber escort missions. In this way, in addition to destroying German fighters caught on the ground, they would cause damage to their maintenance facilities and support units, thereby hastening their demise as an effective force. The combination of attacks in the air and on the ground was to prove disastrous for the *Luftwaffe*, but it was soon found that ground-strafing a defended airfield was a highly dangerous occupation; more American fighter pilots were lost in the ETO to ground-fire than in air combat.

On 6th February, the Thunderbolts of the 78th Fighter Group from Duxford carried out the first mission by Eighth Air Force fighters specifically briefed to attack ground targets with gunfire. At the same time, to encourage the practice of strafing it was announced that in counting personal and unit scores, an enemy aircraft destroyed on the ground would henceforth be given equal credit to an air victory.

In the lead-up to the invasion, certain fighter groups, notably the 355th '*Steeple Morden Strafers*', established a reputation for their prowess in the business of ground attack, perfecting the high-speed low-level techniques developed by the 353rd at Metfield, the self-styled '*Bill's Buzz Boys*' named after VIII Fighter Command's Major General William E Kepner.

The invasion planners had already identified two sets of dates in mid-1944 when the combination of moon and tides would be favourable for landings on the European mainland. The first of these series of dates fell in early May, and was now only three months away. Although the *Luftwaffe* had been suffering an increasing rate of attrition under the guns of Allied fighters, it was still far from defeated. Almost unbelievably, in spite of all its setbacks, at this point the German aircraft industry was still actually increasing its rate of production; it was in terms of pilot availability that the race for air superiority was being won and lost.

Realizing that if the invasion was to go ahead on schedule, it was now becoming a matter of urgency for the German fighter force to be overcome, on 8th February, General Arnold ordered Spaatz to proceed as soon as possible with the planned all-out assault on the German aircraft industry code-named Operation '*Argument*', and to complete it by March 1st.

As so often before, a number of days were to pass before the weather was forecast to be adequate for such a venture. Some months earlier, in anticipation of the crucial role which accurate weather forecasting would play in the success of the major operations planned for 1944, General Arnold had recruited Dr Irving P Krick, in peacetime a meteorologist at the California Institute of Technology, who had developed a controversial method for predicting weather patterns, based on a study of the kind of weather that had occurred in similar conditions in the past.

Some historians have described Operation '*Argument*', or '*Big Week*' as it soon came to be known, as the most significant air battle of the Second World War in that it broke the back of the *Luftwaffe* and allowed the Allied armies to take the first steps on the road to Berlin that summer knowing that airpower was overwhelmingly on their side. It was also one of the few operations in which the Combined Bomber Offensive lived up to its name; on four of the nights of '*Big Week*' the bombers of the RAF mounted raids against targets also attacked by the Eighth Air Force – Leipzig Stuttgart, Schweinfurt and Augsburg – guided through the night by pathfinder flares or by fires started by the Americans during the day.

For most of mid-February East Anglia had been scoured by wind, rain and snow coming in off the North Sea, but on 18th, Krick felt confident to predict the weather window for which Spaatz had been waiting. He forecast that starting on 20th two areas of high pressure would move slowly south-east across Europe bringing at least three days of fair weather to England with the clear skies and good visibility essential for visual precision bombing over Germany. Although this did not guarantee the week-long period that Doolittle needed to deal a decisive blow, with the deadline fast approaching it was decided to seize the opportunity if at all possible. Spaatz gave orders for the bomber and fighter groups to make their final preparations for '*Argument*'.

Krick continued to monitor the developing weather pattern over the following thirty-six hours and on the afternoon of 19th he confirmed his initial assessment. But still the weather remained poor over England; in the circumstances Doolittle and Kepner were reluctant to commit their forces without orders to do so. By the evening Spaatz had considered, consulted and delayed long enough; though conditions were marginal, he announced that the operation was on. Within minutes field orders were going out over the teleprinters to the groups.

Sunday morning 20th February, dawned cloudy with a bitter wind and snow showers over East Anglia. The bombers would have to climb on instruments through 8,000 feet of cloud and assemble in near-darkness; heavy icing was anticipated. There was intense activity before dawn at the airfields of the Eighth Air Force. In preparation for the largest strategic mission yet attempted by any air force, Fortresses and Liberators from sixteen Combat Wings were running up their engines at airfields all over Eastern England. Escort and support was to be provided by fifteen USAAF fighter groups plus fourteen RAF squadrons of Spitfires and two of Mustangs, with diversionary attacks carried out by the medium bombers of the Ninth Air Force.

Over 700 RAF bombers had just returned from their night raid on

Leipzig. Now Big Week was about open with attacks on twelve German aircraft plants, mostly between Brunswick and Leipzig, including the key Erla Me 109 factories near the latter city. For the first time the Eighth Air Force despatched more than 1,000 bombers, supported by the record number of 835 fighters, the Thunderbolts carrying the new 'flat' 150-gallon drop tanks. Almost 11,000 aircrewmen were airborne from the Eighth Air Force alone; coincidentally it was two years to the day since General Eaker had arrived in England with just his 'original six' officers.

With more than forty serviceable bombers on hand and almost as many crews available, at Bassingbourn the 91st prepared to despatch its aircraft in two Groups for the first time – twenty-four bombers forming part of the 1st Combat Wing 'A' formation heading for Leipzig, and eighteen of the older non-Tokyo tank B-17Fs briefed to attack the nearer Junkers components factory at Aschersleben with the 44-strong 1st Wing 'B' box.

The 401st Squadron supplied thirteen crews and eleven aircraft for this mission, five of them for the Aschersleben force – '*Buccaneer*', '*Ramblin' Wreck*', '*Corn State Terror*', '*Quitchurbitchin*' (on loan from the 324th Squadron) and '073, allocated again to Lt Weber's crew, on their seventh mission.

In the event take-off and climb-out were accomplished without incident, followed by formation assembly above the ten-tenths cloudbase. Reconnaissance aircraft returning from dawn flights over Germany reported clear visual conditions for bombing. In an effort to maintain maximum fighter support, the ten Combat Wings in the main force, over 600 bombers of the First and Second Divisions, flew together on the same route to a point west of Brunswick before separating to attack their specific objectives. As the force approached its target area the clouds began to break, but there were not the clear skies above a snow-covered Germany which had been predicted. At more than half of the planned targets visual bombing was possible with excellent results, but as the 1st Wing 'B' box left the main formation in cloudy conditions, it failed to locate Aschersleben and at 1326 hours instead released its load of 500-lb bombs on what was believed to be Oschersleben some twenty five miles away.

The returning 1st Wing crews reported large explosions and fires at the target; the heavy ground fire included a brilliant red five-flare rocket bursting at their altitude, but to no effect. In general their fighter escort was described as fair; in the target area they were supported by the P-38s of the

55th Fighter Group. For the 401st Squadron, enemy fighter opposition was restricted to fifteen aircraft, mostly Fw 190s, attacking out of the haze.

Unlike '073, most of the aircraft in the formation returned from the eight hour mission with some degree of flak damage. Lt Gibbons' crew were flying their twelfth mission in '*Ramblin' Wreck*':

'This concerns the mission of 20.2.44 to Aschersleben, Germany.

I was not at all surprised to see our names on the Alert List. We were flying '679, 'Ramblin' Wreck', and by this time I had a particular feeling for the airplane, a kin-type feeling. I could feel something between the plane and myself. I knew its little idiosyncrasies and its ease of handling and the comfort that I felt in this airplane as opposed to flying in other aircraft. It was not a fast plane. We would rise up at the end of the runway at 175 miles per hour. It was just a good feeling to be in that particular aircraft. I had the same feeling, too, about flying that I've always had. Your heart kind of gets in your mouth and you go through a series of settling down – long breathing – in and out. You don't think of the negative, just that I'm going to do the best job I can. I'm going to encourage everyone around me to perform in the same way and we're going to get the job done.

At briefing, we were told that our target was Oschersleben (sic) and we were briefed as to the activity in the area. There would be some fighters and maybe a concentration of flak here or there, but nothing extreme, nothing that we should be concerned about. We were carrying extra fuel – 410 gallons in the bomb bay tank and 1/2 load of bombs. We'd use the 400 gallons by the time we reached an altitude of 18,000 feet. Breaking over the coast of France, we should concern ourself with having all of our fuel out and prepare to salvo the tanks. On this one mission, I thought that we were (not) going to have enough fuel and I tried to get every drop of gas out of the tank. I asked the co-pilot to scan the gauges and tell me which tank needed a little more fuel so I could get the right adjustment level per load. He checked and I had all the gas out. We were told to dud the tank (fill it with CO_2) and bring it back. I never thought that was a good idea. It seemed to me that it would be a bomb in itself if we didn't do a good job of duding. If a tracer would penetrate that tank, it would explode. I called for the bombardier to open the door and salvo that tank. As I was leaning over trying to unscrew where the hose was connected to the pump, he pulled the release mechanism and the tank fell out. There was a little gasoline left in the hose from the tank to the pump and it covered me with gas. But we got the tank released all right and closed the *bomb bay doors.*

By that time we were over the coast and I had not tested the machine guns yet, so I fired them and everything was in order or seemed to be pretty much in order. We flew in the high composite group. There was an engineer in the airplane next to us. I'd look over and wave to him and he'd wave to me. I always felt comfortable. I thought that if I turned my back on that old boy, he'd take care of me, and I would do the same thing for him. We'd take care of one another. We eventually met some opposition. We didn't have an escort. The opposition flew through the formation, did a little damage, and went back down. We proceeded toward the target and when we got there, the flak was horrible, it was absolutely terrible. The sky was black and the smoke puffs were so close to the airplane that a lot of times they would fill the compartment with smoke. We could actually smell the gunsmoke.

We had a broken undercast and you could see villages, rivers and so forth through the clouds. I always liked that. We finally got to the target and for some reason or other we were in con trails. The windows were frosting up and it was a bit difficult to see where we were going. The waist gunner, Jack Bowen, looked up and right above him was an airplane. He told me later that he could have reached out and shook hands with the ball turret gunner. I looked out and I thought, 'My God', we had slid under the formation. I don't know how in the hell we did that. But anyway, I had just a very small area in front of turret that I could see out of, about the size of a grapefruit or less, with about as much over the top of my head.. Otherwise, it was completely fogged in. I got out of the turret and tapped the pilot on the shoulder, telling him to go down and left – quick, quick, hurry. I looked up and, honest to God, I thought we were going to get caught there. We got out of the way just as the plane above us released its bombs.

Everyone on the plane felt like we had a guardian angel looking out for us that day. We came off the target and it was always kind of spooky at the end of the bomb run. The ground crews would fire a phosphorous bomb and all you could see was it straggling downward. That was a sign for the fighters. Sure enough, there they were. They were very able, very capable pilots.

Every time they came into a formation, they took somebody with them. Their technique was to fly into the formation, invert, and go right down through the formation. And they always got a B-17. We saw several. I saw one B-17 slide off to the side and it was just pathetic. The fighters just came in making real short passes. I saw a burst of fire come out from below and it just completely disintegrated. I didn't see any chutes come out, but some of the other guys said they saw a couple. The only thing that I remember seeing distinctly was a wheel with a strut. It was flying through the air with half of the wing section and motors going like mad. It was a hell of a feeling to see that. I once saw an airplane go out of control and go down and I thought, 'My God, he should pull out'. Well, it looked like there was a feeble attempt to pull out, but it couldn't, and it continued the direct flight down. When it exploded and burned, you could see the smoke coming back up through the undercast.

We were very lucky, we took a lot of holes and we lost the No. 3 engine again. We could not feather it, so we just had to drop back into formation and hope for the best. We had several fighters making passes at us, but we fought like mad. All the guns would shoot in the direction of the fighters. I think it was a case where we made ourselves known and they could not stay up too much longer, so they left. We started back and when we reached the Channel, we just dispersed. We were straggling and we let down into the undercast. There was an element of three airplanes coming through and I don't know how, but we missed colliding. It was a case of thinking that you were going to drive right into a guy's window, but it was just a matter of luck for us again. We got in and landed, happy that sucker was over.

Before the truck came out to pick us up, we were counting holes in the airplane (fuselage). We got to 70-some holes before the truck got there. I noticed a hole right through the damn turret. I don't know how it ever missed me. I don't know where the projectile went or anything. It came through on the right side about where my head would be and apparently it went off the fuselage somewhere. I looked at it and I thought, 'Holy Smolly', we were unbelievably lucky on this raid.

Goecke, the tailgunner, told me about a shell that had burst by the escape hatch back there, blew the lock off, and twisted the door, which didn't fall out. It was a blessing. He said that he thought he'd had it when that happened. It made so damn much noise. But no one was hurt. The thing that always amazed me was when the No. 3 engine was hit, it drained the oil out of the oil cooler and, of course, we couldn't get any pressure to feather the prop, so it just windmilled. It had a tendency to wobble and I've often thought it could have seized up and snapped the top shaft or something and it could have flown through the cabin. It could have severed the cabin. But I was always amazed to think that the damn thing never fell off. We got on the ground and I told the crew chief, 'Let's pull that thing back and forth'. And I'll betcha we moved that thing three feet. It was just absolutely shot. The front end of the engine was scorched. Normally it was grey and now it was brown, because of the heat.

The characteristic of the crew chief was (that) he always wanted to know how the airplane performed, and were there any writeups necessary other than the holes? He was most concerned about it. We could see that they were glad to see us back, but you know in your heart that none of these guys would have gone where we went.'

Of the seven B-17s lost from the First Division only one was from the 91st – 42-29656 '*Skunkface*' of the 322nd Squadron – one of those in the 1st Wing 'B' box Aschersleben force. Taken by surprise in a head-on attack by a lone Fw 190 on the route home, '*Skunkface*' had two engines shot out and was last seen dropping down into the overcast. The pilot Lt Ernest Kidd managed to keep his ship under control long enough for eight of the crew to bail out safely and survive as prisoners of war.

This was not the only act of bravery performed that day, the only mission for which more than one Medal of Honor was awarded to US airmen based in Britain. Three were awarded for almost unbelievable courage displayed by men of the First Division in bringing their shot-up B-17s back to England with wounded and dying crewmates on board. Almost inevitably, two of these awards were posthumous. How much more heroism passed unrecorded in aircraft which then failed to return will never be known.

On balance, the opening round of '*Big Week*' was judged to have been a success. Severe damage had been caused to all of the targets bombed under visual conditions. Out of nearly a thousand bombers entering enemy airspace 880 had bombed effectively, twenty-one had been shot down and one had diverted to land in neutral Sweden. The escort fighters had engaged in countless dogfights to keep the Focke-Wulfs and Messerschmitts away from the bombers, destroying sixty-one enemy aircraft for the loss of only four of their own.

CHAPTER THIRTEEN

LAST MISSION

On the second day of '*Big Week*', the emphasis shifted from the factories of the German aero-industry to the aircraft themselves. The plan for Monday 21st February was for the First Division to bomb three *Luftwaffe* depots and airfields near Munster, the Second Division a large fighter park at Diepholz near Dummer Lake, and the Third Division to repeat the previous day's attack on the Lutter-MIAG Me 110 component factories at Brunswick.

When Field Order Number 287 was received over the teleprinter in the early hours at Bassingbourn and Ridgewell, it directed the 1st Combat Wing to despatch fifty-nine bombers under the call-sign '*Goldsmith Two-One*' to attack an 'important storage depot' for fighters at Gutersloh at 1224 hours BST followed by the 94th 'A' Wing four minutes later.

The 1st Wing under the command of Brig. Gen. Gross was to be led by twenty aircraft of the 381st, with twenty aircraft of the 91st in the low group and a composite 381st/91st high group of twenty-one aircraft. Meanwhile the 40th, 94th 'B' and 41st 'A' and 'B' Wings were to attack similar depots at Lippstadt and Werl.

Take-off was initially scheduled for 0830 and the group and wing formations of the First Division were to join together via St Ives, Ely, Wisbech and Kings Lynn, departing the coast at Cromer at 1012 hours, with the Third Division twelve minutes ahead and the Second Division following sixteen minutes later. Escort on the route out and back was to be provided by four groups of Thunderbolts, with two groups of Lightnings taking over in the target areas, operating with the call-signs of '*Denver Two-One*' through to '*Denver Two-Six*'. The order included the intelligence assessment that there were 675 enemy fighters within a 100-mile radius of the briefed route and target.

After being roused at 0500 hours for breakfast at 0600 and a 0700 briefing, the crews made their way out to the aircraft and began to go through their pre-flight checks; but as the Eighth Air Force prepared to launch another 'maximum effort' they found the weather no better than before. Returning reconnaissance aircraft reported more cloud cover than expected over Western Germany. Take-off had already been postponed by an hour and a half, and while the crews waited impatiently at the dispersals it was delayed by a further half hour, in the hope that conditions in the target area would improve.

The 401st Squadron's complement amounted to six crews, briefed to fly in the first two elements of the nine-ship high squadron of the composite group, the lead and low squadrons being from the 381st Group. The first element consisted of '*Buccaneer*' in the lead position, with '*Corn State Terror*' in No. 2 position on her right and '073 in the No. 3 slot to her left. The pattern was repeated in the second element with '*The Shamrock Special*' leading '*My Beloved Too*' and '*Blue Dreams*', borrowed from the 323rd. Bringing up the rear of the formation was a so-called 'spare' element consisting of another three aircraft of the 323rd – '*Miss Minookie*', '*Miss Ouachita*' and '*Gay Caballeros*'. With their usual B-17, '*Ramblin' Wreck*', out of action because of the damage sustained on the previous day, for their thirteenth mission Lt Gibbon's crew had been allocated '073, an aircraft they had not flown before, but they were still short of a waist gunner.

Ball turret gunner Jack Bowen had flown with Lt Gibbons' crew twice before on '*Ramblin' Wreck*' but on this day he had been detailed to fly as the right waist gunner with Lt Piacentini's crew in '*My Beloved Too*'.

Eventually a jeep passed along the flightline with the order to start engines at 10 am and to await the signal to taxi ten minutes later. Just five minutes before take-off, Sgt Bowen recalls that he was abruptly switched to join Lt Gibbons' crew aboard '073, his place in '*My Beloved Too*' being taken by S/Sgt Richard D Libby. T/Sgt John R Parsons later recorded the preparations for this mission:

'Our name was on the alert board and we were assigned to fly in another airplane, an older airplane. Some people said it was good, I don't know. It was number 073 (Lightning Strikes) and it had had some troubles before, but it was repaired now and flyable.

The crew on this mission was the same except that Conlon was a bombardier replacement for Wendell Quattlebaum and Jack Bowen was serving as a replacement waist gunner for Julius Ginsberg. Jack had flown two other missions with us.

I was just so shocked when I saw our name on the alert list because, the day before, we flew 679 and were absolutely butchered. The thing was just so shattered when we came back, No. 3 engine was gone, and the thing was perforated with holes. I was just surprised we'd be turned around. The crew of 073 was perfectly well. We all slept in the same bay and the crew for that same airplane slept right at our feet. My bed was on the same level as the engineer, whose name was Jim Wood, and Jim was happy to think that we were going to fly that airplane. He had flown it several times. He swore by it. But he said, 'John, let me give you a little tip, my mask for the oxygen system fits all right. What we are going to have to do is trade helmets. You wear my helmet on this flight and give me yours, and in case you don't come back, I will have it'. And I said, 'That's all right'. So we started from that point.

The oxygen system on the 073 was the older type that had a bladder. You would breathe into two or three rubber things about your nose, and as you breathed out, it would expand the bladder. It had a pin in the bladder. If you wanted to pull the pin and blow through it, you could get the moisture out. If you didn't get all the moisture out of the bladder, the damn thing would freeze and freeze solid, and you would quickly have to take it off and reach down inside your zipper jacket, pull out another one and put it on.

We didn't seem all that enthused about flying in the darn thing, but at least we had a job to do and we were going to do it. This plane did have a colourful past. It had a crew that met with all sorts of difficulties. Well, that's the one we picked to fly.

The day before our flight, my turret was hit real bad. The turret started losing hydraulic fluid and it went into the parachute. Of course, that morning I said, 'Do me a favour, will you? Give me an exchange chute'. The airman said, 'Why?' and I said, 'This thing's full of oil'. And he said, 'Go ahead and use it. If it doesn't work, let me know and I'll go ahead and give you another one'. I hated that damn remark because he would say that on the day I had to use it.

We went to our separate corners after briefing. The Jews go in one corner, Protestants go in another corner of the room, and the Catholics go in another. Our priest gives us the Last Rites and Communion. He gives us a blessing and that's *about all. We got up and left.*

We got our bombs from the ground crew and got them in place. Then we got our guns all installed in the cases while waiting for the engine start time. The plane started up good. We taxied out and we would do our runup on the way out. I remember passing Bassingbourn Tower that morning. A priest was standing there and the major officers were waving us off, giving us the 'thumbs up' sign and that sort of thing.

Our mission was an aircraft engine warehouse somewhere in the area of Hanover and the briefing officer always made lightly of the opposition we might meet. 'Oh, I doubt if you'll meet any aircraft at all. There are some in that area. And flak should be slight, you shouldn't have any problem. All this should be damn near a milk run'. Well, you know how that goes.

After preparation, we are ready and taxiing down the runway, getting ready for takeoff. We would taxi down near the runway and wait for another green light, meaning one was going to move up. There were two on the runway then. One plane would move up and the others would fall in behind and we would get in behind in the third position. Each plane would take off thirty seconds after the plane before him, which means we didn't wonder whether it was clear or not as it went down. We accelerated the thing to the firewall and down the runway we'd go, thirty seconds behind the plane in front of us. It was a clear day and we had a good takeoff. It was kind of nice seeing everybody taking the turn at the same rate of climb, same rate of air speed. As we looked on our left, we could see a flare, and that flare was the lead group. We were supposed to get up there and know our position in the formation. We were now headed for our mission.

We were almost to the other side of the Channel. We had to keep climbing to get our designated altitude, which was 25,000 feet. I do know that it was rather cold. We were doing exceptionally well. We had a good formation, a tight box.'

At some point during the long business of formation assembly Lt Weber's crew in '*Blue Dreams*', carrying propaganda leaflets, were obliged to abort the mission with a defective supercharger, thus reducing the 91st contingent to twenty-eight crews; their empty No. 3 slot in the second element was eventually filled by Lt Phil Mack's crew in '*Gay Caballeros*' moving up from the spare element to tack onto the second. Altogether the Eighth Air Force had 924 bombers airborne escorted by 679 fighters. But in the wider picture of the skies over Europe, all was far from well.

The 1st Wing's problems began when, owing to a deviation from the planned route after crossing the North Sea, they failed to rendezvous with their fighter escort over the eastern side of the Zuider Zee (Ijsselmeer) as intended. Thus denied full fighter support but undeterred, the First Division pressed on due east towards Germany with the 1st and 40th Wings leading the 94th 'A' and 'B' and the 41st 'A' and 'B' in staggered pairs, with twelve miles between the head of each pair, the equivalent of four minutes flying time. The orders for the day had required complete radio silence and a ban on the indiscriminate firing of guns. With the exception of one group each in the 94th 'A' and 'B' Wings armed with 100-pounders, all aircraft carried a maximum load of 500-lb GP bombs.

Fifty miles further on the formation moved into German airspace; after another 100 miles the bombers turned south-east and passed to the west of Hannover before swinging round to approach Gutersloh from the east, all the while navigating by 'dead reckoning' of time and distance travelled. As the bomber force neared its target areas in Western Germany many of the wings found their view of the ground obscured yet again by belts of cloud; failing to locate their primary targets, they began to seek secondary targets or even targets of final resort. The majority of the planned targets were in fact attacked but not by the correct groups, and not in the strength intended.

Shortly after 14.00 hours the six wings of the First Division separated to make for their specific targets, and the 1st Wing flew towards Bielefield at a height of 20,000 feet heading for the Initial Point of its attack.

As Gutersloh came into sight through gaps in the cloud, and too late to make an adjustment, the lead crew realized that the 1st Wing was off course for their target. With only moments to spare before bomb release, a decision was taken to abandon the bomb-run and make a full turn over the target area for a second approach.

Among survivors of the mission, opinions are still divided as to where the responsibility lay for that decision, their views varying according to their whereabouts in the formation. Whatever its origin, the manoeuvre effectively sealed the fate of four B-17s in the high squadron of the high composite group, the vulnerable 'Tail End Charlies'.

As the lead ship took the Wing into a tight turn to the left, it entered a bank of cloud, causing the formation to loosen and come apart. Deprived of visual references, the composite group on the outside of the turn was thrown wide like the tail of a whip; the high squadron in particular was scattered, the spare element becoming detached altogether. When the Wing broke out of cloud at the end of its turn, '*Miss Minookie*' and '*Miss Ouachita*' were some distance away from the rest and heading in the wrong direction, towards Minden.

The majority of the German fighters had been held off by the American escort in a fierce dogfight near Steinhuder Lake, but at this precise moment a fighter *Gruppe* which had hitherto been shadowing the 1st Wing swooped down on the high group in a classic attack out of the sun.

Not surprisingly, the available accounts of what happened next are confused; according to the Missing Aircrew Reports, completed after the war, the fighter attack occurred somewhere between Hannover and Munster anytime from noon to 1420 hours at an altitude ranging from 16,000 to 28,000 feet.

Probably more reliable is the post-mission report compiled by the 91st Bomb Group's intelligence officer, Major John H Reid, based on his interrogation of the returning crews, which places the start of the attack to the west of Hannover at 1420 hours. It records that the high squadron was initially subjected to a major attack by twenty to thirty Fw 190s and Me 109s, probably belonging to *Jagdgeschwader* 11 based in the north west of Germany.

Realizing their mistake, the crews of the two 'spare element' ships immediately applied maximum power in an attempt to regain the protection of the formation, but it was not to be. Out on their own '*Miss Minookie*' and '*Miss Ouachita*' had no chance. Ravaged by cannon fire and with crewmen dead and wounded, they quickly dropped away from the formation. '*Miss Minookie*' had become uncontrollable and the survivors bailed out before she hit the ground, the pilot Lt Neal P Ward finally leaving her at a height of only 2,000 feet. Lt Spencer K Osterberg in '*Miss Ouachita*' chose to make a run for it at low level before eventually being brought down near the Dutch border by *Major* Heinz Bär, *Gruppenkommandeur* of II./JG 1 '*Oesau*'.

The onslaught continued in a flurry of high, head-on and tail attacks on the high squadron. Within minutes, all but one of the aircraft in the high squadron had been attacked and two more had been critically damaged – '572 '*My Beloved Too*' and '073 '*Lightning Strikes*'. With his togglier already dead in the nose, Lt Irvin Pracentini took '572 down to tree-top level where after further damage by anti-aircraft fire, he attempted a belly landing, in which both he and his co-pilot received fatal injuries. T/Sgt Libby, who had taken Jack Bowen's place at the right waist gun, and two other crew members were wounded.

T/Sgt John Parsons in the top turret probably had the best overall view of what befell '073:

'They decided at that time, since we were all a little bit off the target, a little bit to the south and to the east, that we should make a 180 and drop, come back across the target, and drop coming across. It sounded like a good idea, and it was, except the lead navigator turned too short. As he did that it completely scattered the formation. Here we were, in a high box or high composite. As we made our turn, we were in a helluva lot of flak, and we were hanging out to dry, so to speak. There were nine airplanes behind ours and two of them I saw blow up immediately. I looked up at the damnedest mess of fighters you ever saw, and they swarmed in like bees. There were a lot of fighters shot down, but we were in a position where we had to fight for our lives. They would come in close and one would be attacking the rear and another would be attacking the right or left side. Most of them came in from the left and, oh my God, we had an Fw 190 come in right over the tail gunner. I told Paul (our communication was good), I said, 'Fight for your life'. And everybody was shooting everything they had. This one plane comes in and I think it was the one that really hurt us. There was a 20-mm explosion in the engine, No. 3 engine. It blew the whole cowling off and three of the jigs on the engine were blown out. You could look down and see the guts just flying around in the engine. Of course, we couldn't feather the darn thing, and when they all started going, it didn't help us at all.

We had a hole in the No. 3 reserve tank and it was as big as a large lamp shade, a helluva of a big hole. Gas was coming on board, it was burning. We had good communication up to a point, but the attacks kept coming. I saw tracers fly through that airplane and I don't know how or why it didn't kill anybody, but it didn't.

I had said that if our communication goes out, we'll ring the bell. And if we hear the bell going constant, get out. At that time, as luck would have it, we lost our communication. The radio was completely dead. Simultaneously, our controls froze. The airplane would go into an attitude of just a slight rate of climb and would shake, jiggle back and forth like it was trying to go, but couldn't go. Paul asked me if it was all right and I got down out of the turret and said, 'I don't think so, it's going to blow'. So Paul rang the bell, and I felt the air come up through the bottom, so I knew the bombardier and navigator were already out. I grabbed the co-pilot and I said, 'Mac, go'. McCallum got down and he was a tall man. There was an area between the seats where he could stand up straight, and he reached over and put on the pilot's parachute, which is a clip-on, and he looked at the number. His number should have been D2, the pilot's was D1 and mine was D5. He looked at the number on that parachute and took it off, and set it right politely in place, reached over and put on his own and turned around. As I previously said, he was a big man and he was sitting right there with his rump sticking up. I stepped on him and he flew right out the hole. I got back up and sat down in the co-pilot's seat and thought, with this thing going like it is and burning like mad, we don't have a ghost of a chance. I told the pilot, 'No, it ain't gonna go, let's get out'. And he said, 'All right, go'. Well, I didn't think he was going to get out, so I got down there by the escape hatch and I waited and waited. He didn't come. So I went back up and I said, 'Are you coming?' And he said, 'Yes, get out'. And I saw his legs come over the seat, down into the opening, and when I saw that, I went out.

All this time I was trying like hell to get my oxygen mask off, and the clip, it was too tight, and it was dragging a long hose. It must have been about six feet long, and it wouldn't come off. I was dragging it along. As I hit the air the sensation was unbelievable. I was right out in the slipstream, just back of the No. 2 engine, which was going full blast. I rolled like a rag doll. I thought my arms were going to be in knots and my legs were going to be in knots. I finally got far enough away from it that, and I don't know why I did, I guess by instinct, but I folded my arms and I put my feet in a diving position. As I looked up, I saw our airplane disappear into the clouds with one hell of an explosion. I saw the pilot then and I saw his chute open. It was then I knew everybody was out.'

As for '073, Sgt Bowen later reflected on how her luck finally ran out:

'Gibbons' crew, including me, were shot down in it the only mission we flew in it. This was Gibbons' crew's thirteenth mission, it seems I had nothing but bad luck that day. The lead navigator did a 360 degree turn over the target, which split our formation, P-47s escorting us had to return to England as they were low on fuel. Then the new (sic) Fw 190's attack out of the sun and shot four B-17s down on the first pass, ours included, we fought the Fw 190s for about twenty minutes, they knocked out our left outboard engine on the first pass and then shot another one out on another pass. The aircraft caught fire, burning badly and with two engines we bailed out, but we gave them quite a battle before bailing out, I got a probable Fw 190 destroyed and I think someone else got one before we left our aircraft.

The pilot was the last one out. He cleared it just before it exploded. He was a brave man. He fought the controls while we bailed out at risk of his own life, quite a man. We spent the next one year and four months as prisoners at Luft VI and Luft IV in Poland.

I can tell you that there is nothing left of 'Lightning Strikes'. The last I saw *of it was an explosion and a ball of fire. The Germans threatened to shoot us as spies because they couldn't find the aircraft we were shot down in.'*

With two engines ablaze ignited and several hundred gallons of fuel remaining in her tanks, it had only been a matter of time before '073 detonated in a giant incandescent flash which consumed the bomber in a fraction of a second. Whatever fragments remained of the B-17 constructed so carefully in California just over a year earlier, tumbled four miles to the ground to join the many other piles of mangled wreckage littering Germany. The debris of '073 fell in open country near the town of Herford; as might be expected, there is no record of any salvage.

Shortly afterwards, all ten crew reached the ground safely and were soon taken into custody. Despite the Wing's second attempt at lining up on its primary target, Gutersloh's airfield remained obscured by overcast and the formation headed north-west towards Osnabruck.

The remaining twenty-four aircraft in the high group were led over the town with the rest of the 1st Wing where they were heavily fired on by the anti-aircraft defences. Beyond Osnabruck the lead crews found a target of opportunity on their course – the airfield at Achmer occupied by a *Luftwaffe* test unit (which was also a primary target for the Second Division) – where they bombed the runways and hangars at 1450 hours through a five-tenths undercast. As the 1st Wing left Germany, several of its aircraft were experiencing problems due to damage by fighters or flak and began to make gradual descents to extend their range, reducing the high squadron to only two ships by the time it reached the Channel.

The 91st Group returned to Bassingbourn by 1705 hours where they were credited with three enemy fighters shot down and three damaged during their battle with the Focke-Wulfs. Of the 861 bombers despatched by the Eighth Air Force, 762 had bombed a target of some description and only fifteen had failed to return. Their escort, which again included two groups of Mustangs, had scored twenty-seven victories at a cost of five fighters lost. Total claims for the day amounted to fifty-one German aircraft destroyed; the tide of events, it seemed, had turned.

The operational life of an aircrew remained perilous, however, right to the very end. Descending through cloud on their return from the mission to Diepholz, two B-17s of the 385th Bomb Group collided over Reedham Marshes in Norfolk shortly before 4 pm and all twenty-one crew members died in the ensuing crash. Captain John N Hutchison's crew had been just minutes from landing at Great Ashfield to complete their twenty-fifth and final mission.

On the following day 41-24490 '*Jack the Ripper*' became the last of the 91st's original complement of B-17s to be lost, when 1st Lt James Considine's crew bailed out near Munster after being savaged by fighters.

CHAPTER FOURTEEN

POSTSCRIPT

And so, '073's part in the Battle of Germany came to an end. For her crew, ahead lay fifteen months of captivity with many hardships to be endured; their Death March from *Stalag Luft* IV in 1945 has been the subject of several published accounts.

'*Big Week*' continued until February 25th, by which time almost 10,000 tons of bombs had been dropped on Germany's aircraft industry. Two additional bomber groups became operational for the last mission of the week, bringing the strength of the Eighth Air Force to thirty, thereby surpassing the number of aircraft available to RAF Bomber Command, and making it the largest air force in the USAAF.

Operation '*Argument*' cost the Eighth Air Force 158 bombers and thirty-three escort fighters, the hardest day being on the 24th when forty-nine bombers were lost. During the same period the *Luftwaffe* lost between 200 and 300 fighters in the air, and hundreds more in the factories and on the ground. More significantly, '*Big Week*' claimed the lives of ninety-nine *Luftwaffe* pilots, with a further sixty-six wounded. Ten days later the Eighth Air Force carried out its first attack on Berlin, the capital of the 'Third Reich'. In circumstances advantageous to itself, the *Luftwaffe* would still be able to inflict significant losses on the Allied bombers for some time to come, notably over Berlin on March 6th, and Nuremberg on March 30/31st, but in retrospect '*Big Week*' can be seen as the turning point in the struggle for air superiority in European airspace. From here on the

Luftwaffe became ever weaker, while the American bombers and their escorts ranging at will over Europe went from strength to strength. In a report to the *Luftwaffe* High Command, General of Fighters Adolf Galland later wrote:

> '*Between January and April 1944 our daytime fighters lost over 1,000 pilots. They included our best Squadron,* Gruppe *and* Geschwader *commanders. Each incursion of the enemy is costing us some fifty aircrew. The time has come when our force is in sight of collapse*'.

As Galland inferred, this position had been reached not only by the destruction of German industry but largely as the result of combat in the air. By attacking the factories and airfields, the bombers obliged the *Luftwaffe* fighters to take to the sky in their defence, where they could be engaged by the American escort.

Just how complete was the process started by '*Big Week*' is illustrated by the fact that on 6th June only two German fighters and a handful of bombers appeared over the Normandy invasion beaches, as against the 15,000 sorties flown in support of the Allies.

The overall effectiveness of the Allied bombing offensive is still a subject of academic debate today, particularly in the light of more recent events. Perhaps the most telling verdict came from the German war production minister Albert Speer when he described the bombers' successes of 1944 as 'the greatest lost battle on the German side'. In response to his postwar interrogation, Speer stated:

> '*The Americans' attacks, which followed a definite system of assault on industrial targets, were by far the most dangerous. It was in fact these attacks which caused the breakdown of the German armaments industry*'.

Back at Bassingbourn Master Sgt Bert Pierce's ground crew were soon given a new bomber to look after; '073's successor was appropriately named '*Spirit of Billy Mitchell*', and survived until 19th April before failing to return from Kassel. Three further aircraft carried the codes 'LL-A' before the end of hostilities – '*The Liberty Run*', '*Sunkist Sue*' and '*Zootie Cutie*'.

Had '073 survived but another month she would almost certainly have returned to the United States; starting in March 1944 the remaining B-17Fs were progressively withdrawn from service and by the end of April

few non-Tokyo tank aircraft were still with the First Air Division. '*Ramblin'*
Wreck', '*Buccaneer*', '*Corn State Terror*' and '*The Shamrock Special*' were all
returned to Air Force Service Command via the Base Air Depot at
Burtonwood, and relegated to training duties. Their replacements,
B-17Gs, many in the new natural metal finish, were welcomed not only
for the uprated nose armament but also for their electrically-controlled
superchargers; loss of power due to failure of its hydraulic supercharger
controls at high altitude had been a persistent problem with the B-17F.

The 91st Bomb Group flew its 340th and last mission of the war on 25th
April, 1945, and began to depart from Bassingbourn just over a month
later. While stationed in England the 91st had flown 9,591 sorties and been
credited with destroying 420 enemy aircraft, but 197 of their own aircraft
and crews had failed to return, a greater loss than any other bomb group in
the Eighth Air Force; of these the 401st Squadron suffered the highest
losses in the group with fifty-seven missing aircraft. With an average
strength of about twelve aircraft this represented the attrition of the whole
squadron almost five times over in the space of less than three years. By the
war's end 960 aircrewmen of the 91st were prisoners of war, and over 1,000
had been killed or remained missing in action.

At its peak strength the Eighth Air Force consisted of forty-one bomber
groups, of which twenty-one were equipped with the B-17, and fifteen
fighter groups, and numbered nearly a quarter of a million personnel. Its
total losses were more than four thousand bombers and over two thousand
fighters, with some 43,000 airmen killed or missing.

Through all their tribulations and in the face of terrible losses the Eighth
Air Force, unfettered by rigid military attitudes, displayed a 'can-do' spirit
of dogged independence and commitment to their task, and embodied the
proud tradition that no American bomber force sent into battle has ever
been turned back by enemy action; after all, these were men whose
pioneering ancestors had left their homelands and crossed an ocean to
make their way in the New World.

Of the fifteen crews which were assigned to fly in '073 at one time or
another, almost all subsequently lost members killed, missing in action or
taken prisoner. The names of 161 airmen appear on the crew lists for '073's
ferry flight to the UK and her twenty-seven combat missions. Of these,
twenty were killed in action, twelve were posted as missing in action and
forty-one became prisoners of war. Eighty-eight crewmen, just over half of

the total, completed their combat tours, two of them after surviving ditchings in the sea. The only crew of '073 to survive intact was that of Lt Roy Griesbach, who flew their final mission to Ludwigshafen on 27th May, 1944, in the ship they had named '*The Jub Jub Bird*'. Lt Howard Weber's crew almost made it in one piece, all but one of its members making their thirtieth missions on various dates from 8th May onwards; tail gunner Jack Paget had become separated from the rest and was flying his twenty ninth mission with another crew aboard '*The Liberty Run*' when she was shot down on 20th July. Along with many thousands of PoWs, Jack was repatriated by mid-1945.

After the war a few of '073's crew members remained in the US Air Force, like James H McPartlin who had been promoted to CO of the 401st Squadron during 1944, and later rose to the rank of Brigadier General. Jack Bowen transferred to an aerial photography unit and eventually retired in the rank of Master Sergeant, becoming a top instructor in martial arts. He finally received his Purple Heart Medal at a ceremony in his hometown of Carthage, Texas in 1997, fifty-three years after the event.

Jack's lifelong friend John R Parsons was discharged at the war's end but enlisted in the USAF reserve and was recalled to duty with the 434th Troop Carrier Group at Fort Benning, Georgia during the Korean War. He eventually retired as vice-president of a finance company. After an interval of more than fifty years, in 1995 John flew with the 'Triangle A' once more when The Collings Foundation's B-17G, painted to represent '*Nine-O-Nine*' of the 323rd Squadron, visited Purdue University Airport at Lafayette. On landing he said 'It was a thrill to last a lifetime'. He died in 1998. Both Jack and John made several trips to Europe during the 1980s, revisiting Bassingbourn en route, to find the surrounding countryside, if not the towns, little changed. Jack Bowen was among the 4,000 veterans present at the opening of the American Air Museum in Britain by HM the Queen in 1997.

Jack Paget was honourably discharged from the USAAF in September 1945. He re-enlisted in 1947 and eventually retired in 1965 with the rank of Senior Master Sergeant. He returned to his home town of Pasadena, California and worked for the Correctional System and the United States Postal Service before starting his own accounting business which he later passed to his eldest son. Jack hosted the 91st Bomb Group Memorial Association reunion in San Diego, California in 1980.

Bill Gibbons flew on as an airline pilot, and later became president of the North-East Division of United Airlines.

Wilfred Conlon graduated from Boston University in 1948 and became the senior partner of a law firm in Chicopee, Massachusetts. Prior to his death in 1996, in response to this study, Wilf kindly pulled out papers and documents that he had not looked at for many years. 'It has been', he wrote, 'like a trip down memory lane'.

Bert J Pierce became foreman of the Modoc Pear Orchard at Table Rock, Oregon and later worked for the Jackson County Road Department, retiring in 1975. His daughter remembers that at airshows he could always tell where a particular B-17 had been built simply by the pattern or number of its rivets. He died in 1998.

Having returned briefly at the time of the Korean emergency, the Americans finally left Bassingbourn in 1951 and the base was handed back to the RAF. After more than a decade as a Canberra Operational Conversion Unit, regular flying ceased there in 1969. Unlike many former airfields which quickly returned to farmland, Bassingbourn became an army camp, first as Headquarters of the Queen's Division and since 1993 as the home of the Army Training Regiment.

Much of the base is still easily recognizable to the American veterans who visit from time to time and are welcomed as honoured guests. Three of the four hangars still stand, the 401st's having been demolished as unsafe in 1995. The rest are in daily use, as fitness centres and drill halls, along with most of the original buildings.

Since 1975, the control tower has housed an excellent museum operated by volunteers of the East Anglian Aviation Society. The barracks blocks and 'pilot houses' are still in use and the old football pitch is now a drill square. Part of the main runway and most of the perimeter track and dispersals are much as they were in 1944, including those used by the 401st Squadron, now within the 'outdoor training area'. It is still possible to walk the same loop hardstandings once occupied by '073 and her sister-ships; nearby are the shooting-in butts, now used as a small-arms range.

The 91st Bomb Group is well-remembered at Bassingbourn; a sign on the village green bears the image of a bomber in flight and just inside the main gate of the former USAAF Station 121, at the site of annual commemorative ceremonies, a B-17 propeller is mounted as a permanent memorial to the outstanding Bomb Group which was based there for almost a thousand days. The base's initial recruit training unit is now proudly named 'Wray Company' in honour of the 91st's first commanding officer, and outside the recruits' social club the signboard proclaims its name – '*Memphis Belle*'.

At Road Farm to the north of the base, the farmer's family can still recall the names on the bombers which used to sit at the 322nd Squadron dispersals just beyond their farmyard. In the local pubs, photographs of American aircraft and their crews still adorn the walls. There are no battlefields to be visited in the sky and so old airfields often become the focus for memories of departed airmen; for many, an airfield was the scene of their last earthly contact. So it is at Steeple Morden where the site of the former fighter base is marked by a magnificent monument featuring the nose and propeller of a Mustang.

Little Staughton, Ludham, Ridgewell, Deenethorpe, Nuthampstead and Old Buckenham have all shrunk to shadows of their former selves, but are still used as airstrips for private flying. The latter four all have impressive memorials to the bomber groups which once flew from them. Brampton Grange is now a comfortable hotel, Wycombe Abbey has long since resumed its role as a leading girls school and Bushy Park has once again become home only to a herd of royal deer. At the head of Whitchurch's fast-disappearing runway stands a pillar in memory of the wartime Air Transport Auxiliary.

In all, about forty-five B-17s have been preserved, most of them in the USA, thousands having been broken up for scrap metal after the war. Of the 100 or so Fortresses allocated to the 401st Squadron between 1942 and 1945, remarkably, one survives; B-17G 42-32076 '*Shoo Shoo Shoo Baby*' was assigned in March 1944 and completed twenty-three missions with the squadron as 'LL-E' before her crew were obliged to seek refuge in Sweden after sustaining flak damage on the approach to Poznan on 29th May. Remaining in Sweden after the war, she later served as an airliner in Denmark and an aerial-mapping ship in France. In 1971 she was donated to the US Air Force Museum as a wreck for the sum of one *franc* and fully restored, including having the nose-art repainted by the original artist, Tony Starcer. The most famous B-17 of all, and the only other surviving combat veteran, '*Memphis Belle*' of the 324th Squadron, was also preserved and is displayed under a purpose-built dome at the Mud Island Leisure Complex in Memphis, Tennessee. In 1996, the Mighty Eighth Air Force

Heritage Museum was opened just outside Savannah, Georgia where it all began.

The Eighth Air Force still operates the most powerful bomber fleet in the world, which includes the B-1 Lancer and stealthy B-2 Spirit. From time to time its bombers are again seen in the English countryside when the international situation requires B-52s to be deployed to the giant airbase at Fairford in Gloucestershire. Boeing Field at Seattle is still the home of the world's leading commercial planemaker, and also the base of the Museum of Flight's B-17 42-29782, one of the only three surviving F models. The Boeing Aircraft Company still retain their rights and responsibilities as manufacturer of the Flying Fortress; as recently as October 2001 an Airworthiness Directive was issued grounding all fifteen of the world's flying B-17s until their wing spars and the sixty-four attachments bolts had been checked or replaced after cracks had been found in one of them. Happily, all but one were later cleared to resume operations.

Three B-17s can still be seen in England, two on static display and one airworthy, and all of them in markings familiar to the crews of '073. 44-83735, restored to represent '*Mary Alice*' of the 401st Bomb Group, is now a centrepiece of the American Air Museum at Duxford alongside later models in Boeing's series of heavy bombers, the larger B-29 Superfortress and gigantic B-52 Stratofortress. The Royal Air Force Museum's Bomber Hall at Hendon displays 44-83868 in the 'Square A' colours of the 94th Bomb Group next to examples of its one-time adversaries, the Me 109 and the Fw 190, and its escort the P-51 Mustang. The famous 44-85784 '*Sally B*', operated by B-17 Preservation, has flown to the delight of air show audiences for many years; since playing a lead role in the remake of '*Memphis Belle*' in 1989 she has flown from her Cambridgeshire base in markings of the 91st Bomb Group.

The Missions & Crews of 42-3073

17th April – 22nd April 1943

Ferry flight from US to UK via Northern Ferry Route.

Pilot	1st Lt	Harold A Johnson	KIA	13.6.43
Co-Pilot	2nd Lt	Henry A Kvevli	KIA	13.6.43
Bombardier	2nd Lt	Blair Hale	KIA	13.6.43
Navigator	2nd Lt	David C Fussell	KIA	13.6.43
Engineer	Tech. Sgt	Ambrose A Chott	KIA	13.6.43
Asst. Engineer	Staff Sgt	Carl S Cook	KIA	13.6.43
Radio Op./Gunner	Tech. Sgt	Edmond M Hamic	KIA	13.6.43
Ball Turret Gunner	Sgt	Allen W Danaher	KIA	13.6.43
Gunner	Staff Sgt	Winston E Love	KIA	13.6.43
A/Gunner	Staff Sgt	Harold H Derouchie	KIA	13.6.43

Crew No. 'M-46' of 94th Bomb Group. Shot down on Mission No. 9 (Kiel).

Wednesday 15th September 1943

91BG Mission 72   8AAF Mission 95   Romilly-sur-Seine

P	2nd Lt	Robert A Pitts	KIA	3.11.43
CP	2nd Lt	Kenneth B Rutledge	MIA	3.11.43
N	2nd Lt	James P McAvoy	KIA	3.11.43
B	2nd Lt	Julian M Hexum		
E	T/Sgt	F J Parkerson		
R	T/Sgt	Ross L Repp	PoW	10.10.43
BTG	S/Sgt	Antone L Pacheco	KIA	3.11.43
RWG	S/Sgt	Edwin P Mason	KIA	3.11.43
LWG	Sgt	Robert L Youker		
TG	S/Sgt	Donald J Aldrich		

Bomb load	: 38 x 100-lb IB
Casualties	: None
Damage	: None
Time over target	: 1848 hrs
Altitude	: 23,000 ft
Crews despatched by 91st BG	: 19
Crews despatched by 401st BS	: 2

B-17F 42-3073	'LL-A'	*'Lightning Strikes'*	2nd Lt	Robert A Pitts
B-17F 42-29591	'LL-Z'	*'The Shamrock Special'*	Capt.	Harry T Lay

Thursday 23rd September 1943

91BG Mission 74   8AAF Mission 100   Nantes

P	2nd Lt	Robert A Pitts	KIA	3.11.43
CP	2nd Lt	William B Smith		
N	2nd Lt	Ralph A Villanova		
B	2nd Lt	Julian M Hexum		
E	T/Sgt	Forrest G Seaver		
R	S/Sgt	Milton Rallis		
BTG	S/Sgt	Antone L Pacheco	KIA	3.11.43
RWG	S/Sgt	Edwin P Mason	KIA	3.11.43
LWG	Sgt	John W Montgomery	KIA	3.11.43
TG	S/Sgt	Donald J Aldrich		

Bomb load	: 12 x 500-lb GP
Casualties	: None
Damage	: M/gun damage
Time Over Target	: 0818 hrs
Altitude	: 21,000 ft
Crews despatched by 91st	: 21
Crews despatched by 401st	: 4

B-17F 42-29591	'LL-Z'	*'The Shamrock Special'*	Capt. Harry T Lay
B-17F 42-29679	'LL-A1/M'	*'Ramblin' Wreck'*	2nd Lt Hilary H Evers Jr
B-17F 42-29793	'LL-F'	*'Sheila B Cummin'*	2nd Lt Millard H Jewett Jr
B-17F 42-3073	'LL-A'	*'Lightning Strikes'*	2nd Lt Robert A Pitts

Saturday 2nd October 1943

91BG   Mission 77   8AAF Mission 106   Emden

P	1st Lt	Charles R Phillips	PoW	22.3.44
CP	2nd Lt	William B Smith		
N	2nd Lt	Grey C Winchester	MIA	3.11.43
B	2nd Lt	Jerome D Pope		
E	Sgt	Lawrence P Yenchik	PoW	3.11.43
R	T/Sgt	E W Koprowski (324BS)		
BTG	Sgt	Chester R Zimmerman	PoW	22.3.44
RWG	S/Sgt	Robert L Jackson	PoW	22.3.44
LWG	S/Sgt	Anthony Dannucci Jr	PoW	22.3.44
TG	S/Sgt	Elvin Walsh	PoW	22.3.44

Bomb load	: 42 x 100-lb IB, 1 x 1,000-lb GP
Casualties	: None
Damage	: None
Time over target	: 1615 hrs
Altitude	: 22,000 ft
Crews despatched by 91st	: 16
Crews despatched by 401st	: 4

B-17F 41-24484	'LL-C'	*'Bad Egg'*	Capt. Harry T Lay
B-17F 42-3073	'LL-A'	*'Lightning Strikes'*	1st Lt Charles R Phillips
B-17F 42-29793	'LL-F'	*'Sheila B Cummin'*	2nd Lt Earle R Verrill
B-17F 42-5729	'LL-E'	*'Buccaneer'*	Capt. Eugene M Lockhart

Friday 8th October 1943

91BG Mission 79   8AAF Mission 111   Bremen

P	1st Lt	Charles R Phillips	PoW	22.3.44
CP	2nd Lt	William B Smith		
N	2nd Lt	Grey C Winchester	MIA	3.11.43
B	2nd Lt	Thomas W Kenefick	MIA	3.11.43
E	T/Sgt	Marion E Painter	PoW	22.3.44
R	S/Sgt	Victor H Kuhlmann	PoW	14.10.43
BTG	Sgt	Chester R Zimmerman	PoW	22.3.44
RWG	S/Sgt	Robert L Jackson	PoW	22.3.44
LWG	S/Sgt	Anthony Dannucci Jr	PoW	22.3.44
TG	S/Sgt	Elvin Walsh	PoW	22.3.44

Bomb load	: 10 x 500-lb GP
Casualties	: B wounded
Damage	: Cat. A flak damage
Time over target	: 1505 hrs
Altitude	: 24,000 feet
Crews despatched by 91st	: 16
Crews despatched by 401st	: 5 (2 aborted)

B-17F 42-29591 'LL-Z'	*'The Shamrock Special'*	Capt. Eugene M Lockhart(ab)
B-17F 42-3060 'LL-G'	*'Hell's Belle'*	1st Lt Hilary H Evers Jr
B-17F 42-29679 'LL-A1/M'	*'Ramblin' Wreck'*	1st Lt Millard H Jewett Jr(ab)
B-17F 42-30805 'LL-H'	*'Bomb Boogie's Revenge'*	1st Lt Robert A Pitts
B-17F 42-3073 'LL-A'	*'Lightning Strikes'*	1st Lt Charles R Phillips

Saturday 9th October 1943

91BG   Mission 80   8AAF Mission 113   Anklam

P	1st Lt	Hilary H Evers Jr		
CP	2nd Lt	Robert S Roberts		
N	2nd Lt	Bruce D Moore		
B	2nd Lt	Charles S Hudson		
E	T/Sgt	James A Wood		
R	T/Sgt	John J Alba		
BTG	S/Sgt	Gilbert L Taft	PoW	10.10.43
RWG	S/Sgt	Troy C Young		
LWG	S/Sgt	Ernest P Colvin	PoW	3.11.43
TG	S/Sgt	Leonard L Gibbs		

Bomb load   : 3 x 1,000-lb GP, 5 x IB
Casualties   : B wounded
Damage   : Cat. C; major
Time over target   : 1144 hrs
Altitude   : 12,500 ft
Claims   : 3 credited
Crews despatched by 91st   : 17
Crews despatched by 401st   : 5 (3 aborted)

B-17F 42-5729   'LL-E'   *'Buccaneer'*   1st Lt Robert A Pitts(ab)
B-17F★ 42-3506   'LL-?'   *'Sir Baboon McGoon'* 1st Lt Charles R Phillips(ab)
B-17F 42-29679   'LL-A1/M' *'Ramblin' Wreck'*   1st Lt Millard H Jewett Jr
B-17F 42-3073   'LL-A'   *'Lightning Strikes'* 1st Lt Hilary H Evers Jr
B-17G 42-37737   'LL-K'   *'Tennessee Toddy'*   2nd Lt Earle R Verrill(ab)

★but configured as B-17G (chin turret)

Wednesday 20th October 1943

91BG Mission 83   8AAF Mission 116   Duren

P	1st Lt	Kenneth B Rutledge	MIA	3.11.43
CP	2nd Lt	William B McAdams	MIA	3.11.43
N	2nd Lt	Grey C Winchester	MIA	3.11.43
B	2nd Lt	Thomas W Kenefick	MIA	3.11.43
E	T/Sgt	Samuel W Allender	MIA	3.11.43
R	T/Sgt	Alfred Ramones	MIA	3.11.43
BT	Sgt	Chester R Zimmerman	PoW	22.3.44
RWG	S/Sgt	Gilberto M Ortiz	MIA	3.11.43
LWG	Sgt	Clarence E Edwards	PoW	3.11.43
TG	S/Sgt	Earl V. Miller	MIA	3.11.43

Bomb load	: 500-lb GP
Casualties	: BTG sick
Damage	: None
Time over target	: Early return
Altitude	: N/A
Crews despatched by 91st	: 3
Crews despatched by 401st	: 3

B-17F 42-3073 'LL-A' *'Lightning Strikes'*   1st Lt Kenneth B Rutledge

B-17F 42-30805 'LL-H' *'Bomb Boogie's Revenge'* 1st Lt Robert A Pitts

B-17F 42-3060 'LL-G' *'Hell's Belle'*   1st Lt Millard H Jewett Jr

Friday 5th November 1943

91BG Mission 85   8AAF Mission 121   Gelsenkirchen

P	1st Lt	Hilary H Evers Jr		
CP	2nd Lt	Robert S Roberts		
N	2nd Lt	Bruce D Moore		
B	2nd Lt	Wilfred P Conlon	PoW	21.2.44
E	Sgt	Milton Rallis		
R	T/Sgt	John A Capron		
BTG	S/Sgt	Chester R Zimmerman	PoW	22.3.44
RWG	Sgt	Leon W Bryant		
LWG	Sgt	Junior H Clifton		
TG	S/Sgt	Troy C Young		

Bomb load	: 42 x 100-lb IB
Casualties	: None
Damage	: Cat. A flak damage
Time over Target	: 1344 hrs
Altitude	: 28,500 ft
Crews despatched by 91st	: 18
Crews despatched by 401st	: 2 (plus 1 aborted)

B-17F 41-24484	'LL-C'	*'Bad Egg'*	Capt. Eugene M Lockhart
B-17F 42-3073	'LL-A'	*'Lightning Strikes'*	1st Lt Hilary H Evers Jr
B-17F 42-29679	'LL-A1/M'	*'Ramblin' Wreck'*	aborted

Sunday 7th November 1943

91BG Mission 86   8AAF Mission 124   Wesel

P	1st Lt	Charles R Phillips	PoW	22.3.44
CP	2nd Lt	William B Smith		
N	Lt	Julian M Hexum		
B	Lt	James A Graham	PoW	29.3.44
E	T/Sgt	William C Darden	ditched	17.8.43
RG	T/Sgt	Winfield B Neal		
BTG	S/Sgt	Chester R Zimmerman	PoW	22.3.44
RWG	S/Sgt	Robert L Jackson	PoW	22.3.44
LWG				
TG	S/Sgt	Anthony Dannucci Jr	PoW	22.3.44

Bomb load	: 500-lb GP / 100-lb IB
Casualties	: None
Damage	: No. 4 engine fault
Time over target	: Early return
Altitude	: N/A
Crews despatched by 91st	: 18
Crews despatched by 401st	: 2

B-17F 42-3073	'LL-A'	*'Lightning Strikes'*	1st Lt Charles R Phillips
B-17F 42-3060	'LL-G'	*'Hell's Belle'*	1st Lt Millard H Jewett Jr

Tuesday 16th November 1943

91BG Mission 87	8AAF Mission 131	Knaben

P	1st Lt	Millard H Jewett Jr		
CP	F/O	Paul G McDuffee		
N	1Lt	John W Ryan	PoW	22.4.44
B	Capt.	J W Maupin (401BG)		
E	T/Sgt	Winfield B Neal		
R	T/Sgt	Warren F King		
BTG	S/Sgt	Joseph York		
RWG	S/Sgt	Elmer Weaver		
LWG	S/Sgt	Steve P Resko		
TG	S/Sgt	Frederick H Lenke Jr		

Bomb load	: 8 x 500-lb GP, 20 x IB.
Casualties	: None
Damage	: None
Time Over Target	: Abortive sortie
Altitude	: N/A
Crews despatched by 91st	: 20
Crews despatched by 401st	: 4

B-17F 42-5729	'LL-E'	*'Buccaneer'*	Capt. James H McPartlin
B-17F 42-3073	'LL-A'	*'Lightning Strikes'*	1st Lt Millard H Jewett Jr
B-17G 42-37767	'LL-D'		1st Lt Hilary H Evers Jr
B-17F 42-5795	'LL-B'	*'Skoal'*	2nd Lt Julius D C Anderson

Friday 26th November 1943

91BG Mission 88   8AAF Mission 138   Bremen

P	2nd Lt	Julius D C Anderson	KIA	29.3.44
CP	2nd Lt	Horace C Nichols		
N	2nd Lt	Joe G Stuart	PoW	29.3.44
B	2nd Lt	James A Graham	PoW	29.3.44
E	S/Sgt	Jewel C Maddox	MIA	29.3.44
R	S/Sgt	Donald R Bartlett		
BTG	S/Sgt	Derwood A Briggs		
RWG	S/Sgt	Maurice F Skiles		
LWG	S/Sgt	Albert G Romulis		
TG	S/Sgt	Aldrich A Seeley	MIA	29.3.44

Bomb load	: 8 x 500-lb GP, 20 x IB
Casualties	: None
Damage	: Cat. A flak damage
Time over target	: 1220 hrs
Altitude	: 26,000
Crews despatched by 91st	: 29
Crews despatched by 401st	: 6 (plus 2 aborted)

B-17G 42-31079	'LL-J/F'		2nd Lt Charles A Guinn
B-17F 42-3073	'LL-A'	*'Lightning Strikes'*	2nd Lt Julius D C Anderson
B-17F 42-29679	'LL-A1/M'	*'Ramblin' Wreck'*	2nd Lt William F Gibbons
B-17G 42-31187	'LL-F/K'	*'Buckeye Boomerang'*	2nd Lt John D Davis
B-17F 42-5795	'LL-B'	*'Skoal'*	2nd Lt Bob Tibbetts Jr (ditched)
B-17G 42-39771	'LL-H'	*'Jeannie Marie'*	2nd Lt Frank D Turk
B-17G 42-37767	'LL-D'		aborted
B-17F 42-5729	'LL-E'	*'Buccaneer'*	aborted

Sunday 5th December 1943

91BG Mission 90　　　　8AAF Mission 149　　　　Paris

P	Capt.	James H McPartlin	(Sqn Ops)
CP	Col	Clemens K Wurzbach	(Gp CO)
N	Capt.	S M Slaton	(Gp Nav.)
B	Lt	Bruce D Moore	
E	T/Sgt	William C Darden	ditched 17.8.43
R	T/Sgt	Ted R Cetnarowski	ditched 17.8.43
BTG	S/Sgt	Maurice F Skiles	
RWG	S/Sgt	Donald J Aldrich	
LWG	T/Sgt	Forrest G Seaver	
TG	2nd Lt	Frank L Butler	PoW　11.4.44

Bomb load	: 500-lb GP, 100-lb IB
Casualties	: None
Damage	: None
Time over target	: Abortive sortie
Altitude	: 24,000 ft
Crews despatched by 91st	: 10
Crews despatched by 401st	: 4

B-17F 42-3073　'LL-A'　*'Lightning Strikes'*　　　　Capt. James H McPartlin
B-17F 41-24639　'OR-W'　*'The Careful Virgin'* (323BS)　Lt Julius D C Anderson
B-17F 42-5729　'LL-E'　*'Buccaneer'*　　　　Lt Charles R Phillips
B-17G 42-37736　'DF-G'　*'Duke of Paducah'* (324BS)　Lt William F Gibbons

Saturday 11th December 1943

91BG Mission 91   8AAF Mission 151   Emden

P	Lt	Charles L Price		
CP	Lt	Philip R Goynes		
N	Lt	Howard A Groombridge		
B	Lt	Lee D Godfrey		
E	Sgt	Ward E Simonson		
R	Sgt	Robert J Jackson		
BTG	Sgt	Freeman A Ford		
RWG				
LWG	S/Sgt	John Hinda		
TG	Sgt	Hugh E Winfree	PoW	19.4.44

Bomb load   : 41 x 100-lb IB
Casualties   : None
Damage   : None
Time over target   : 1243 hrs
Altitude   : 22,500 ft
Crews despatched by 91st   : 24
Crews despatched by 401st : 6 (plus 1 aborted)

B-17G 42-31187	'LL-F/K'	*'Buckeye Boomerang'*	Lt John D Davis
B-17G 42-39771	'LL-H'	*'Jeannie Marie'*	Lt Frank D Turk
B-17G 42-31079	'LL-J/F'		Lt Paris R Coleman
B-17G 42-37767	'LL-D'		Lt Robert S Roberts
B-17F 42-29679	'LL-A1/M'	*'Ramblin' Wreck'*	Lt William F Gibbons
B-17F 42-3073	'LL-A'	*'Lightning Strikes'*	Lt Charles L Price
B-17F 42-5729	'LL-E'	*'Buccaneer'*	aborted

Monday 13th December 1943

91BG Mission 92   8AAF Mission 154   Bremen

P	2nd Lt	Irvin Piacentini	KIA	21.2.44
CP	Lt	J B Britton III		
N	2nd Lt	Bernard P Hart	PoW	21.2.44
B	2nd Lt	Frederick W Merkert		
E	S/Sgt	Fred R Kirby		
R	S/Sgt	Robert E Gerstemeier		
BTG	Sgt	Samuel L Sommers	PoW	19.4.44
RWG	Sgt	Robert S Miller	PoW	21.2.44
LWG	Sgt	Robert M Dodge	KIA	21.2.44
TG	Sgt	Glenn G Selter	PoW	21.2.44

Bomb load	: 42 x 100-lb IB
Casualties	: None
Damage	: Cat. A flak damage
Time over target	: 1204 hrs
Altitude	: 28,000 ft
Crews despatched by 91st	: 31
Crews despatched by 401st	: 9

B-17F 41-24484	'LL-C'	*'Bad Egg'*		Capt. James H McPartlin
B-17F 41-24505	'DF-C'	*'Quitchurbitchin'* (324BS)		Lt Frank D Turk
B-17F 42-5804	'LG-R'	*'Hell's Halo'* (322BS)		Lt William F Gibbons
B-17G 42-31187	'LL-F/K'	*'Buckeye Boomerang'*		Lt John D Davis
B-17F 42-5279	'LL-E'	*'Buccaneer'*		Lt Charles R Phillips
B-17G 42-39771	'LL-H'	*'Jeannie Marie'*		Lt Frank C Armann
B-17G 42-37767	'LL-D'			Lt Charles L Price
B-17F 42-3073	'LL-A'	*'Lightning Strikes'*		Lt Irvin Piacentini
B-17G 42-31079	'LL-J/F'			Lt Paris R Coleman

Thursday 16th December 1943

91BG Mission 93   8AAF Mission 156   Bremen

P	Lt	Julius D C Anderson	KIA	29.3.44
CP	Lt	Horace C Nichols		
N	Lt	Joe G Stuart	PoW	29.3.44
B	Lt	James A Graham	PoW	29.3.44
E	S/Sgt	Jewel C Maddox	MIA	29.3.44
R	T/Sgt	Andrew Beluschak	PoW	29.3.44
BTG	S/Sgt	Albert G Romulis		
RWG	S/Sgt	Donald R Bartlett		
LWG	PFC	Harold R Harding	PoW	21.2.44
TG	S/Sgt	Aldrich A Sealey	MIA	29.3.44

Bomb load	: 8 x 500-lb GP, 18 x IB
Casualties	: None
Damage	: Cat. A m/gun damage
Time over target	: 1312 hrs
Altitude	: 24,500 ft
Crews despatched by 91st	: 27
Crews despatched by 401st	: 6

B-17F 41-24505	'DF–C'	*'Quitchurbitchin'* (324BS)	Lt Hilary H Evers Jr
B-17F 42-3073	'LL-A'	*'Lightning Strikes'*	Lt Julius D C Anderson
B-17G 42-31187	'LL-F/K'	*'Buckeye Boomerang'*	Lt John D Davis
B-17F 42-5729	'LL-E'	*'Buccaneer'*	Lt Charles R Phillips
B-17G 42-31079	'LL-J/F'		Lt Paris R Coleman
B-17G 42-37767	'LL-D'		Lt Charles L Price

Monday 20th December 1943

91BG Mission 94   8AAF Mission 159   Bremen

P	Lt	William B Smith		
CP	Lt	George H Heilig		
N	Lt	William P Richards		
B	F/O	Thomas J Capparell		
E	T/Sgt	James A Wood		
R	T/Sgt	Fred R Kirby		
BTG	Sgt	Martin Goldberg	MIA	29.3.44
RWG	S/Sgt	Frank Topitz		
LWG	Sgt	Kenneth F Fiigen	PoW	19.4.44
TG	Sgt	Paul C Bara		

Bomb load	: 12 x 500-lb GP
Casualties	: None
Damage	: None
Time over target	: 1147 hrs
Altitude	: 27,600 ft
Crews despatched by 91st	: 27
Crews despatched by 401st	: 7

B-17F 41-24484	'LL-C'	*'Bad Egg'*	Lt Hilary H Evers Jr
B-17G 42-31079	'LL-J/F'		Lt Paris R Coleman
B-17F 42-3073	'LL-A'	*'Lightning Strikes'*	Lt William B Smith
B-17F 42-5729	'LL-E'	*'Buccaneer'*	Lt Robert S Roberts
B-17F 42-29679	'LL-A1/M'	*'Ramblin' Wreck'*	Lt Charles L Price
B-17G 42-31187	'LL-F/K'	*'Buckeye Boomerang'*	Lt Bob Tibbetts Jr
B-17G 42-37767	'LL-D'	(write-off)	Lt Howard F Weber

Friday 31st December 1943

91BG Mission 98   8AAF Mission 171   Bordeaux (Cognac)

P	Lt	Julius D C Anderson	KIA	29.3.44
CP	Lt	Horace C Nichols		
N	Lt	Harold A Levin		
B	Lt	Patrick H McNulty	PoW	11.4.44
E	T/Sgt	Jewel C Maddox	MIA	29.3.44
R	T/Sgt	Andrew Beluschak	PoW	29.3.44
BTG	Sgt	Chester R Zimmerman	PoW	22.3.44
RWG	S/Sgt	Donald R Bartlett		
LWG	Sgt	Kenneth F Fiigen	PoW	19.4.44
TG	S/Sgt	Aldrich A Seeley	MIA	29.3.44

Bomb load   : 21 x M47 IB

Casualties   : None

Damage   : None

Time over target   : 1305 hrs

Altitude   : 18,000 ft

Crews despatched by 91st : 32

Crews despatched by 401st : 9

B-17F 41-24484	'LL-C'	*'Bad Egg'*	Lt Hilary H Evers Jr
B-17F 42-3057	'LG-N'	*'Blonde Bomber'* (322BS)	Lt John E La Fontin
B-17F 42-29741	'LL-D'	*'Corn State Terror'*	Lt Robert S Roberts
B-17F 42-29679	'LL-A1/M'	*'Ramblin' Wreck'*	Lt William F Gibbons
B-17F 42-5804	'LG-R'	*'Hell's Halo'* (322BS)	Capt James H McPartlin
B-17F 42-29591	'LL-Z'	*'The Shamrock Special'*	Lt William B Smith
B-17F 42-3073	'LL-A'	*'Lightning Strikes'*	Lt Julius D C Anderson
B-17G 42-31079	'LL-J/F'		Lt Paris R Coleman
B-17G 42-31187	'LL-F/K'	*'Buckeye Boomerang'*	Lt John D Davis

Tuesday 4th January 1944

91BG Mission 99   8AAF Mission 174   Kiel

P	2nd Lt	Uwell W McFarland		
CP	2nd Lt	Thomas H Gunn		
N	2nd Lt	Paolino Santacrose		
B	2nd Lt	Harold P Johnson		
E	S/Sgt	David S McCall		
R	Sgt	Rollie C Hill		
BTG	Sgt	George R Zenz	MIA	3.2.45
RWG	Sgt	James F Lonergan		
LWG	Sgt	John J Dias	PoW	22.2.44
TG	Sgt	Delbert R Lowry		

Bomb load	: 42 x M47 IB
Casualties	: None
Damage	: Minor flak damage
Time over target	: 1138 hrs
Altitude	: 26,000 + ft
Crews despatched by 91st	:
Crews despatched by 401st	: 6

B-17G 42-39771	'LL-H'	*'Jeannie Marie'*		Lt Robert S Roberts
B-17G 42-39929	'LL-K/X'	*'Lackin' Shackin'*		Lt Frank C Amman
B-17G 42-31578	'LL-L'	*'My Darling Also'*		Lt William B Smith
B-17G 42-31187	'LL-F/K'	*'Buckeye Boomerang'*		Lt Bob Tibbetts Jr
B-17G 42-31079	'LL-J/F'			Lt Paris R Coleman
B-17F 42-30712	'OR-O/R	*Miss Minookie* (323BS)		Lt William F Gibbons

Crews despatched by 324th :   4 (plus 3 aborted)

B-17F 42-29739	'OR-M'	*'The Village Flirt'*(323BS)	1st Lt Kenneth V Kerr
B-17G 42-37779	'DF-B'	*'Pistol Packin' Mama'*	2nd Lt Allen A Uskela (ab)
B-17F 42-30773	'DF-B/J'		1st Lt Marco DeMara (ab)
B-17F 41-24490	'DF-A'	*'Jack the Ripper'*	2nd Lt Harvey G Hesse
B-17F 42-3073	'LL-A'	*'Lightning Strikes'*(401BS)	Lt Uwell W McFarland
B-17G 42-31230	'DF-A1'	*'Little Jean'*	2nd Lt John Klotz (ab)
B-17F 42-29837	'DF-A'	*'Lady Luck'*	Lt Fred E Knight

Wednesday 5th January 1944

91BG Mission 100   8AAF Mission 176   Tours

P	Lt	Julius D C Anderson	KIA	29.3.44
CP	Lt	Horace C Nichols		
N	Lt	Joe G Stuart	PoW	29.3.44
B	Lt	Donald T Weiss		
E	S/Sgt	Samuel L Sommers Jr	PoW	19.4.44
R	T/Sgt	Andrew Beluschak	PoW	29.3.44
BTG	S/Sgt	Albert G Romulis		
RWG	S/Sgt	Donald R Bartlett		
LWG	S/Sgt	Neil Gillis	PoW	20.3.44
TG	S/Sgt	Aldrich A Seeley		

Bomb load	: 16 x 300-lb GP
Casualties	: None
Damage	: Cat. A flak damage
Time over target	: 1144 hrs
Altitude	: 20,500 ft
Crews despatched by 91st	:
Crews despatched by 401st	: 8

B-17F 41-24639 'OR-W'	*'The Careful Virgin'* (323BS)	Capt. James H McPartlin
B-17G 42-31187 'LL-F/R'	*'Buckeye Boomerang'*	Lt Roy J Griesbach
B-17G 42-37958 'LL-G'	*'Old Faithful'*	Lt Charles L Price
B-17G 42-31578 'LL-L'	*'My Darling Also'*	Lt Robert S Roberts
B-17G 42-39771 'LL-H'	*'Jeannie Marie'*	Lt Lester F Rentmeester
B-17F 42-29679 'LL-A1/M'	*'Ramblin' Wreck'*	Lt Sam L Evans
B-17F 42-3073 'LL-A'	*'Lightning Strikes'*	Lt Julius D C Anderson
B-17G 42-39929 'LL-K/X'	*'Lackin' Shackin'*	Lt Frank C Amman

Friday 7th January 1944

91BG Mission 101   8AAF Mission 178   Ludwigshafen

Pos	Rank	Name	Status	Date
P	1st Lt	Julius D C Anderson	KIA	29.3.44
CP	2nd Lt	Horace C Nichols		
N	1st Lt	Joe G Stuart	PoW	29.3.44
B	1st Lt	James A Graham	PoW	29.3.44
E	T/Sgt	Jewel C Maddox	MIA	29.3.44
R	T/Sgt	Andrew Beluschak	PoW	29.3.44
BTG	S/Sgt	Albert G Romulis		
RWG	S/Sgt	Neil Gillis	PoW	20.3.44
LWG	S/Sgt	Norman V Pero	PoW	20.3.44
TG	S/Sgt	Aldrich A Seeley	MIA	29.3.44

Bomb load	: 8 x 250-lb IB
Casualties	: None
Damage	: None
Time over target	: 1157 hrs
Altitude	: 27,000 ft
Claims	: Me 109 destroyed, Me 109 probable
Crews despatched by 91st	:
Crews despatched by 401st	: 5 (plus 1 aborted)

B-17G 42-31578 'LL-L'	*'My Darling Also'*	Lt Charles R Phillips	
B-17G 42-39929 'LL-K/X'	*'Lackin' Shackin''*	Lt John E LaFontin	
B-17G 42-37958 'LL-G'	*'Old Faithful'*	Lt Charles L Price	
B-17F 42-3073 'LL-A'	*'Lightning Strikes'*	Lt Julius D C Anderson	
B-17F 42-29679 'LL-A1/M'	*'Ramblin' Wreck'*	Lt Roy J Griesbach	
B-17G 42-39771 'LL-H'	*'Jeannie Marie'*	aborted	

Tuesday 11th January 1944

91BG Mission 102   8AAF Mission 182   Oschersleben

P	2nd Lt	Roy J Griesbach
CP	2nd Lt	Charles R Peck
N	2nd Lt	John R Simonson
B	2nd Lt	John H Piland
E	T/Sgt	Emil J Viskocil
R	S/Sgt	Robert G Hartford
BTG	S/Sgt	Ralph E Rigaud
RWG	S/Sgt	Harry V Lane
LWG	S/Sgt	Harry R Small
TG	S/Sgt	John D Hamner
Bomb load	: 21 x 100-lb IB	
Casualties	: None	
Damage	: None	
Time over target	: 1147 hrs	
Altitude	: 21,000 ft	
Claims	: 3 destroyed	
Crews despatched by 91st	: 31	
Crews despatched by 401st	: 9 (plus 1 aborted)	

B-17G 42-31187	'LL-F/K'	*'Buckeye Boomerang'*	1st Lt John D Davis
B-17F 42-5729	'LL-E'	*'Buccaneer'*	Capt. James H McPartlin
B-17G 42-39929	'LL-K/X'	*'Lackin' Shackin'*	2nd Lt Frank C Amman
B-17G 42-39771	'LL-H'	*'Jeannie Marie'*	2nd Lt Lester F Rentmeester
B-17F 42-29591	'LL-Z'	*'The Shamrock Special'*	1st Lt Robert S Roberts
B-17F 42-29679	'LL-A1/M'	*'Ramblin' Wreck'*	2nd Lt Sam L Evans
B-17G 42-31079	'LL-J/F'		2nd Lt Paris R Coleman
B-17G 4231578	'LL-L'	*'My Darling Also'*	1st Lt William B Smith
B-17G 42-37958	'LL-G'	*'Old Faithful'*	1st Lt Bob Tibbetts Jr (ab)
B-17F 42-3073	'LL-A'	*'Lightning Strikes'*	2nd Lt Roy J Griesbach

Saturday 29th January 1944

91BG Mission 105   8AAF Mission 198   Frankfurt

P	2nd Lt	Howard F Weber		
CP	2nd Lt	John C Flinn Jr		
N	2nd Lt	Earl R Hedstrom		
B	2nd Lt	Donald T Weiss		
E	S/Sgt	Willis J Kaltenbach		
R	S/Sgt	Louis R Holland		
BTG	Sgt	Russell R Ruth		
RWG	S/Sgt	James R Marshall		
LWG	S/Sgt	Eugene R Letalien		
TG	S/Sgt	John R Paget	PoW	20.7.44

Bomb load	: 21 x 100-lb IB
Casualties	: None
Damage	: None
Time over target	: c. 1200 hrs
Altitude	: 23,800 ft
Crews despatched by 91st	:
Crews despatched by 401st	: 13

B-17F 42-5729	'LL-E'	*'Buccaneer'*	Capt James H McPartlin
B-17G 42-38006	'DF-H'	*'Hoosier Hot Shot'* (324BS)	1st Lt Julius D C Anderson
B-17G 42-31578	'LL-L'	*'My Darling Also'*	1st Lt William B Smith
B-17G 42-31572	'LL-Y'	*'My Beloved Too'*	1st Lt Bob Tibbetts Jr
B-17F 42-29679	'LL-A1/M'	*'Ramblin' Wreck'*	1st Lt William F Gibbons
B-17F 42-3073	'LL-A'	*'Lightning Strikes'*	2nd Lt Howard F Weber
B-17G 42-39929	'LL-K/X'	*'Lackin' Shackin'*	1st Lt Frank C Amman
B-17F 42-29591	'LL-Z'	*'The Shamrock Special'*	1st Lt Roy J Griesbach
B-17G 42-31672	'LL-?'	*'Buckeye Boomerang II'*	1st Lt John D Davis
B-17G 42-37911	'LL-C'	*'The Heats On'*	1st Lt Sam L Evans
B-17G 42-37958	'LL-G'	*'Old Faithful'*	1st Lt Charles L Price
B-17G 42-31079	'LL-J/F'		1st Lt Paris R Coleman
B-17G 42-39771	'LL-H'	*'Jeannie Marie'*	1st Lt Frank D Turk

Sunday 30th January 1944

91BG Mission 106   8AAF Mission 200   Brunswick

P	2nd Lt	Howard F Weber		
CP	2nd Lt	John C Flinn Jr		
N	2nd Lt	Earl R Hedstrom		
B	2nd Lt	Donald T Weiss		
E	S/Sgt	Willis J Kaltenbach		
R	S/Sgt	Louis R Holland		
BTG	Sgt	Russell R Ruth		
RWG	S/Sgt	James R Marshall		
LWG	S/Sgt	Eugene R Letalien		
TG	S/Sgt	John R Paget	PoW	20.7.44

Bomb load	: 6 x 500-lb GP
Casualties	: None
Damage	: Cat. A m/gun damage
Time over target	: 1158 hrs
Altitude	: 22,300 ft
Claims	: Me 109 destroyed, Fw 190 probable
Crews despatched by 91st	:
Crews despatched by 401st	: 6

B-17G 42-31079	'LL-J/F'		1st Lt Frank C Amman
B-17G 42-31578	'LL-L'	*'My Darling Also'*	1st Lt William B Smith
B-17F 42-3073	'LL-A'	*'Lightning Strikes'*	2nd Lt Howard F Weber
B-17F 42-5729	'LL-E'	*'Buccaneer'*	1st Lt Charles R Phillips
B-17F 42-29591	'LL-Z'	*'The Shamrock Special'*	2nd Lt Irvin Piacenti
B-17G 42-37958	'LL-G'	*'Old Faithful'*	1st Lt Charles L Price

Thursday 3rd February 1944

91BG Mission 107	8AAF Mission 206	Wilhelmshaven

P	1st Lt	Julius D C Anderson	KIA	29.3.44
CP	2nd Lt	Horace C Nichols		
N	Lt	Joe G Stuart	PoW	29.3.44
B	F/O	James A Graham	PoW	29.3.44
E	T/Sgt	Jewel C Maddox	MIA	29.3.44
R	T/Sgt	Andrew Beluschak	PoW	29.3.44
BTG	S/Sgt	Albert G Romulis		
RWG	Sgt	Jack S Bowen	PoW	21.2.44
LWG	S/Sgt	Kenneth P Fiigen	PoW	19.4.44
TG	S/Sgt	Aldrich A Seeley	MIA	29.3.44

Bomb load	: 6 x 500-lb GP
Casualties	: None
Damage	: None
Time over target	: 1124 hrs
Altitude	: 28,000 ft
Crews despatched by 91st	: 30
Crews despatched by 401st	: 6

B-17F 42-5729	'LL-E'	*'Buccaneer'*	1st Lt Charles R Phillips
B-17F 42-29741	'LL-D'	*'Corn State Terror'*	Lt Clyde V Mason
B-17F 42-29591	'LL-Z'	*'The Shamrock Special'*	2nd Lt Irvin Piacentini
B-17F 42-3073	'LL-A'	*'Lightning Strikes'*	1st Lt Julius D C Anderson
B-17G 42-31672	'LL-?'	*'Buckeye Boomerang II'*	2nd Lt James R Lutz
B-17G 42-39929	'LL-K/X'	*'Lackin' Shackin'*	1st Lt Frank C Amman

Friday 4th February 1944

91BG Mission 108   8AAF Mission 208   Frankfurt

P	1st Lt	William B Smith		
CP	2nd Lt	George H Heilig		
N	1st Lt	William P Richards		
B	F/O	Thomas J Capparell		
E	T/Sgt	James A Wood		
R	T/Sgt	Andrew Beluschak	PoW	29.3.44
BTG	S/Sgt	Harold R Harding	PoW	21.2.44
RWG	S/Sgt	Neil Gillis	PoW	20.3.44
LWG	S/Sgt	Norman V Pero	PoW	20.3.44
TG	S/Sgt	Paul C Bara		

Bomb load	: 6 x 500-lb GP
Casualties	: None
Damage	: None
Time over target	: 1205 hrs
Altitude	: 26,000 ft
Crews despatched by 91st	: 33
Crews despatched by 401st	: 8 (plus 1 aborted)

B-17F 42-5729 'LL-E'	*'Buccaneer'*	1st Lt Charles R Phillips
B-17F 42-29591 'LL-Z'	*'The Shamrock Special'*	1st Lt Lester F Rentmeester
B-17G 42-38027 'LG-A'	*'Heavenly Body'* (322BS)	Lt Clyde V Mason
B-17F 42-3073 'LL-A'	*'Lightning Strikes'*	1st Lt William B Smith
B-17G 42-31079 'LL-J/F'		1st Lt Paris R Coleman
B-17G 42-37911 'LL-C'	*'The Heat's On'*	Lt Roy J Griesbach
B-17G 42-39929 'LL-K/X'	*'Lackin' Shackin'*	Lt Howard F Weber
B-17G 42-39771 'LL-H'	*'Jeannie Marie'*	2nd Lt James R Lutz MIA
B-17G 42-31572 'LL-Y'	*'My Beloved Too'*	aborted

Sunday 6th February 1944

91BG Mission 110   8AAF Mission 212   Nancy-Essey

P	2nd Lt	Irvin Piacentini	KIA	21.2.44
CP	2nd Lt	James A Rogers	KIA	21.2.44
N	2nd Lt	Bernard P Hart	PoW	21.2.44
B	2nd Lt	Frederick W Merkert		
E	S/Sgt	Richard D Libby	PoW	21.2.44
R	T/Sgt	John L Wolstenholme	PoW	21.2.44
BTG	S/Sgt	Harold J Rhode	KIA	6.3.44
RWG	S/Sgt	Robert S Miller	PoW	21.2.44
LWG	S/Sgt	Robert M Dodge	KIA	21.2.44
TG	S/Sgt	Glenn G Selter	PoW	21.2.44

Bomb load	: 500-lb / 1,000-lb GP
Casualties	: None
Damage	: None
Time over target	: Abortive sortie
Altitude	: N/A
Crews despatched by 91st	: 33
Crews despatched by 401st	: 9

B-17F 42-29591	'LL-Z'	*'The Shamrock Special'*	1st Lt Hilary H Evers Jr
B-17G 42-37911	'LL-C'	*'The Heat's On'*	1st Lt Roy J Griesbach
B-17G 42-31572	'LL-Y'	*'My Beloved Too'*	1st Lt Bob Tibbetts Jr
B-17G 42-31672	'LL-?'	*'Buckeye Boomerang II'*	1st Lt John D Davis
B-17G 42-39929	'LL-K/X'	*'Lackin' Shackin'*	1st Lt Frank C Amman
B-17F 42-3073	'LL-A'	*'Lightning Strikes'*	2nd Lt Irvin Piacentini
B-17F 42-29679	'LL-A1/M'	*'Ramblin' Wreck'*	1st Lt Lester F Rentmeester
B-17F 41-24505	'DF-C'	*'Quitchurbitchin'* (324BS)	1st Lt Julius D C Anderson
B-17F 41-24504	'DF-D'	*'The Sad Sack'* (324BS)	1st Lt Sam L Evans

Sunday 20th February 1944

91BG Mission 112   8AAF Mission 226   Aschersleben (Oschersleben)

P	2nd Lt	Howard F Weber		
CP	2nd Lt	John C Flinn Jr		
N	2nd Lt	Earl R Hedstrom		
B	2nd Lt	Donald T Weiss		
E	T/Sgt	Willis J Kaltenbach		
R	T/Sgt	Louis R Holland		
BTG	S/Sgt	Russell R Ruth		
RWG	S/Sgt	James R Marshall		
LWG	S/Sgt	Eugene J Letalien		
TG	S/Sgt	John R Paget	PoW	20.7.44

Bomb load	: 6 x 500-lb GP
Casualties	: None
Damage	: None
Time over target	: 1326 hrs
Altitude	: 14,200 ft
Crews despatched by 91st	: 42
Crews despatched by 401st	: 13

B-17F 42-29591	'LL-Z'	*'The Shamrock Special'*	Lt Robert S Roberts
B-17G 42-39929	'LL-K/X'	*'Lackin' Shackin'*	1st Lt Frank G Ammann
B-17G 42-31079	'LL-J/F'		1st Lt Charles R Phillips
B-17G 42-37911	'LL-C'	*'The Heat's On'*	2nd Lt Irvin Piacentini
B-17G 42-31572	'LL-Y'	*'My Beloved Too'*	1st Lt Lester F Rentmeester
B-17F 41-24505	'DF-O'	*'Quitchurbitchin'* (324BS)	1st Lt Bob Tibbetts Jr
B-17F 42-3073	'LL-A'	*'Lightning Strikes'*	2nd Lt Howard F Weber
B-17G 42-37958	'LL-G'	*'Old Faithful'*	1st Lt Charles L Price
B-17G 42-31578	'LL-L'	*'My Darling Also'*	1st Lt Sam L Evans
B-17F 42-5729	'LL-E'	*'Buccaneer'*	1st Lt Paris R Coleman
B-17F 42-29679	'LL-A1/M'	*'Ramblin' Wreck'*	1st Lt William F Gibbons
B-17G 42-37736	'DF-G'	*'Duke of Paducah'* (324BS)	1st Lt Roy J Griesbach
B-17F 42-29741	'LL-D'	*'Corn State Terror'*	1st Lt Frank D Turk

Monday 21st February 1944

91BG Mission 113	8AAF Mission 228	Gutersloh (Achmer)

P	1Lt	William F Gibbons	PoW	21.2.44
CP	2Lt	Clyde P McCallum	PoW	21.2.44
N	1Lt	Donald E Shea	PoW	21.2.44
B	1Lt	Wilfred P Conlon	PoW	21.2.44
E	T/Sgt	John R Parsons	PoW	21.2.44
R	T/Sgt	William O Douponce	PoW	21.2.44
BTG	Sgt	Clarence R Bateman	PoW	21.2.44
RWG	Sgt	Jack S Bowen	PoW	21.2.44
LWG	S/Sgt	Julius W Edwards	PoW	21.2.44
TG	S/Sgt	Paul H Goecke	PoW	21.2.44

Bomb load	: 12 x 500-lb GP
Casualties	: 10 crew PoW
Damage	: Missing in Action
Time over target	: –
Altitude	: 20,000 ft
Claims	: Fw 190 probable
Crews despatched by 91st	: 29
Crews despatched by 401st	: 6 (1 aborted)

B-17F 42-5729	'LL-E'	*'Buccaneer'*	1st Lt Charles R Phillips
B-17F 42-29741	'LL-D'	*'Corn State Terror'*	1st Lt Frank C Ammann
B-17F 42-3075	'LL-A'	*'Lightning Strikes'*	1st Lt William F Gibbons MIA
B-17F 42-29591	'LL-Z'	*'The Shamrock Special'*	1st Lt Paris R Coleman
B-17G 42-31572	'LL-Y'	*'My Beloved Too'*	2nd Lt Irvin Piacentini MIA
B-17G 42-37761	'OR-L'	*'Blue Dreams'* (323BS)	2nd Lt Howard F Weber(ab)

Select Bibliography

Action Stations : Volume 1	M J F Bowyer	Patrick Stevens	1979
Airfields of the Eighth Then and Now	R A Freeman	After the Battle	1978
Air War Europa	E Hammel	Pacifica	1994
B-17 Flying Fortress	H P Willmott	Bison	1981
B-17 Flying Fortress	J Ethell	Arms & Armour	1986
B-17 Flying Fortress	M W Bowman	Crowood	2000
The B-17 Flying Fortress	R Jackson	MBI/Spellmount	2001
B-17 Flying Fortress Units of the 8th Air Force	M Bowman	Osprey	2000
B-17 Fortress at War	R A Freeman	Allan	1977
Battle Stations	Downing/Johnston	Leo Cooper	2000
The Best Seat in the House	J R Parsons		1998
Big Week	G Infield	Pinnacle Books	1974
Black Thursday	M Caidin	E P Dutton	1960
The Boeing B-17 E & F	C D Thompson	Profile Pub.	
The Boeing B-17 G	R A Freeman	Profile Pub.	
Boeing B-17 Flying Fortress	M W Bowman	Crowood	1998
The Bomber Command War Diaries	Middlebrook & Everitt	Viking	1985
The Bomber Offensive	A Verrier	Batsford	1968
Bomber Offensive: the Devastation of Europe	N Frankland	Macdonald	1970

Castles in the Air	M W Bowman	Patrick Stephens	1984
Combat Crew	J Comer	Leo Cooper	1988
Combat Squadrons of the Air Force in World War II		USAF Hist. Divn	1969
Crusade in Europe	D D Eisenhower	Heinemann	1948
Deadly Sky	J C McManus	Presidio	1999
Decision over Schweinfurt	T M Colley	Hale	1978
Destiny's Child	J R Paget	Pilot Publication	1978
The Eighth Air Force Story	K C Rust	Hist. Aviation Album	1978
Final Flights	I McLachlan	Patrick Stephens	1989
The First and the Last	A Galland	Methuen & Co	1955
Flying to Glory	M W Bowman	Patrick Stephens	1992
Fortress Without a Roof	W H Morrison	W H Allen	1982
Fortresses of the Big Triangle First	C T Bishop	East Anglia Books	1986
General Billy Mitchell	R Burlingame	McGraw-Hill	1952
The GIs; the Americans in Britain	N Longmate	Hutchinson & Co	1975
History of 91st BG: Report to Members	H H Evers	91BGMA	1990
Lingering Contrails of the Big Square 'A'	H E Slater		1980
Lion in the Sky	J Scutts	Patrick Stephens	1987
The Lost Command	A Revie	David Bruce & Watson	1971
Luftwaffe: Strategy for Defeat	W Murray	George Allen & Unwin	1985
The Luftwaffe War Diaries	C Bekker	Macdonald	1967
The Mighty Eighth	R A Freeman	Macdonald	1972
Mighty Eighth War Diary	R A Freeman	Janes	1981
Mighty Eighth War Manual	R A Freeman	Janes	1984
Once There Was a War	J Steinbeck	Heinemann	1959
Pilot Training Manual for the Flying Fortress		USAAF	1944
Plane Names & Fancy Noses	R Bowden	Design Oracle Part.	1993
The Ragged Irregulars of Bassingbourn	Havelaar/Hess	Schiffer	1995
A Real Good War	S Halpert	Southern	1997

		Heritage/Cassell	
The Schweinfurt — Regensburg Mission	M Middlebrook	Allen Lane	1993
The Role of the Bomber	R W Clark	Sidgwick & Jackson	1977
Schweinfurt: Disaster in the Skies	J Sweetman	Ballantine	1971
Serenade to the Big Bird	B Stiles	Lindsay Drummond	1947
Strategic Air Offensive against Germany	Webster/Frankland	HMSO	1961
The Struggle for Europe	C Wilmot	Collins	1952
Target Berlin	J Ethell/A Price	Janes	1981
Target Germany	HMSO	London	1944
The Tibbetts Story	P W Tibbetts	Stein & Day	1978
1942: The Turning Point	A Wykes	Macdonald	1972
Vintage Aircraft Nose Art	G M Valant	Motorbooks Int.	1987
Wings of Judgement	R Schaffer	Oxford Univ Press	1985